Indianapolis Museum of Art
Collections Handbook

Indianapolis Museum of Art
Collections Handbook

RT

Published by the
Indianapolis Museum of Art, Indianapolis, Indiana
1988

708
IND

Contents

All measurements are in inches (centimeters),
height precedes width precedes depth.

Foreword

A handbook of a museum's collections is intended to provide an overview of its holdings for the general public. The many people who have contributed to this handbook have had this goal in mind, and it is their hope that this publication fully meets that purpose. In a sense the IMA *Handbook* is a reflection in miniature of our collections, and this volume, with its numerous illustrations and accompanying informative texts, will serve as an introduction to those collections. The *Handbook* is also a statement in time, that is, a selection which includes both works of art acquired many years ago and some shortly before publication. I am certain that just as the *Handbook* sees the light of day new and important works will come to the Museum. Undoubtedly, these will be included in future editions.

This book is a result of many years of growth that began with two modest paintings in 1883, the Museum's first year. In the ensuing years the collections have increased to nearly 40,000 works that encompass the history of world art. From this very large number, the authors of the *Handbook* have chosen a representative sampling with the hope that from their selections you will be able to gain a true sense of our holdings. This has not been an easy task! This publication was also very complex from a logistical point of view. I would like to thank Holliday Day, Curator of Contemporary Art, who has served as general editor, for keeping us all moving and for seeing to the assembling of all materials in final form for publication.

To the members of the Alliance of the Indianapolis Museum of Art, who have helped underwrite this project financially, go my thanks without measure not only for their assistance with this publication, but also for their generous donations of time and money to so many Museum activities. The Indianapolis Museum of Art is truly fortunate to have the tremendous support of the Alliance volunteers.

The National Endowment for the Arts has also provided financial assistance for this project. Over the years the grants from this federal agency have been vital to many of our Museum programs. We are again deeply grateful for their generous support.

Finally, I would like to express my deepest gratitude to the hundreds of donors of works of art, or of funds to purchase them, throughout all the years of the Museum's history. The *Handbook* is dedicated to them.

Robert A. Yassin
Director

Acknowledgments

The publication of a book such as this one, covering an enormous range of works of art, can be achieved only through a major effort on the part of the staff, especially the curatorial staff, both past and present. The following people participated in the selection process and wrote many of the entries that accompany the illustrations: Robert A. Yassin, Director; Peggy S. Gilfoy, Curator of Textiles and Ethnographic Arts; Martin F. Krause, Jr., Associate Curator of Prints and Drawings; Ellen Wardwell Lee, Curator of Painting and Sculpture; James J. Robinson, Curator of Oriental Art; A. Ian Fraser, Research Curator for the Clowes Collection; Amanda Austin, former Assistant Curator of Decorative Arts; and Joanne M. Kuebler, Assistant Director of Education for Academic Affairs.

This book would not have been possible without the two former Chief Curators of the Museum: Anthony F. Janson, who began the work on the *Handbook* as an outgrowth of his earlier *100 Masterpieces of Painting: Indianapolis Museum of Art*, written with Ian Fraser; and Hollister Sturges, who carried the project forward, wrote many of the entries, and under whose supervision the majority of the work was accomplished. Genetta Gardner, formerly Museum Intern and now Assistant Curator of Painting at the Cincinnati Art Museum, provided enormous assistance to Mr. Sturges in organizing the material and wrote many entries.

Finally, credit should be given to authors Jane Ju, former Museum Intern in Oriental Art, and Hsing-li Tsai, the current Museum Intern in Oriental Art; former Museum Photographer Melville D. McLean for his superb photography; Marcia A. Palmer, for her patient and careful typing of the manuscript; and Margaret B. Bradbury, Museum Editor, for her assistance in seeing the *Handbook* through the press. To all of my colleagues above, I extend my thanks for making my task as easy as possible.

Holliday T. Day
General editor

European Collection

Christ's Entry into Jerusalem, c. 1125
Fresco transferred to canvas
70¾ x 121 (179.6 x 307.4)
Gift of G. H. A. Clowes and Elijah B. Martindale 57.151

Christ's Entry into Jerusalem and its companion piece at the IMA, *The Marriage at Cana*, are a part of a cycle devoted to the miracles and Passion of Christ from the early twelfth-century Romanesque mozarabic church, San Baudelio, near Berlanga, Spain. The remote location and relative inaccessiblity of the church contributed to the survival of eight paintings of the cycle over the centuries until their dispersal in the 1920s to American and European collections, including the IMA, the Metropolitan Museum of Art, the Museum of Fine Arts Boston, the Cincinnati Art Museum, and the Prado, Madrid.

This painting represents the early Romanesque style prevalent in France and northern Spain during the twelfth century. Characteristic of the period are life-size figures, inscribed with curvilinear decorative patterning, that extend the entire height of the composition; the emphasis on surface decoration through flat, schematic drapery folds; and the rhythmic repetition of the earth-colored figures that creates an abstract design.

Agnolo Gaddi, c. 1350-1396
Saint Mary Magdalen in the Wilderness, Saints Benedict,
Bernard of Clairveaux, and Catherine of Alexandria, c. 1390
Tempera on panel
28½ x 8 (72 x 22) each panel
Clowes Fund Collection

These four standing saints were probably part of a large altarpiece
that included a panel of the enthroned Virgin and Child. In fact,
the close connection of the figures of three of the saints (Benedict,
Bernard, and Catherine) to those in the *Madonna and Child En-*
throned with Angels and Saints Andrew, Benedict, Bernard, and
Catherine, of about 1390, at the National Gallery in Washington
suggests that the panels were part of a similar polyptych, close in
date to the one at the National Gallery. The style of the figures is
typical of Gaddi's work in the late fourteenth century, which is
characterized by clear, vivid color, substantial, three-dimension-
ally modeled forms, and large soft folds of drapery. This style
dominated the Late Gothic period in Florence, from the late fourteenth century to the early fifteenth century.

Furnishing or garment fabric, c. 1475 (detail)
Silk velvet weave with silk supplementary warp and metallic
supplementary weft (pile-on-pile and voided velvet with brocade)
80 x 24 (203.5 x 60.5)
Roger G. Wolcott Fund 82.7

The swirling "pomegranate" design, here in gold threads with blue silk velvet, has antecedents in ancient Middle Eastern and Chinese patterns. The design probably made its first appearance in Venice, which was particularly well suited to the development of such luxury goods because of its extensive trade with the Near East. The large scale of the pattern seems to indicate its use on furnishings or walls, but contemporary paintings also document similar silks used in garments. The rare blue, which is not an ecclesiastical color, suggests a secular function.

Ewer stand, c. 1510-20
Tin-glazed earthenware (majolica)
16⅛ (41.6) diam.
Daniel P. Erwin Fund 59.21

The clearest indication of the Sienese origin of this stand is the decoration on the back, a radial flower with striped petals expanding around the base. On the face the numerous concentric borders, colored with a dark red known as *terra di Siena*, are further distinguishing elements. The filling motifs of arabesques and scales create an effect of flat patterns, although the central portion has a raised boss that conforms to the base of the lost ewer. Before the widespread use of cutlery, the scented water that filled the ewer was used for washing hands between courses.

Neroccio de' Landi, 1447-1500
*Madonna and Child with Saints John the Baptist and
Mary Magdalen*, c. 1496
Tempera on panel
28 x 20⅛ (71 x 51)
Clowes Fund Collection

Half-length images of the Madonna and Child flanked by saints
were popular subjects in Siena during the fifteenth century and
were especially beloved by the Sienese painter, Neroccio de' Landi.
Neroccio created a number of variations on the theme, and this
painting, along with its counterpart at the Metropolitan Museum
of Art, New York, numbers among his finest late masterpieces.
Our painting is particularly distinguished for its preservation of
thin translucent layers of surface color that are no longer intact in
many other paintings by Neroccio. While the plump proportions
of the Christ Child reveal that Neroccio was receptive to the Florentine style of the fifteenth century, the slender, tapered forms of
the female figures and the lightness and variation of color reveal
the artist's more decorative tastes, which are indicative of the
Sienese school.

Giuliano Bugiardini, 1475-1554
Madonna and Child with the Infant Saint John the Baptist,
c. 1508-10
Oil on panel
34¼ (87) diam.
Gift of Mr. and Mrs. William H. Ball 79.1133

The Madonna and Child with the infant Saint John in a landscape is a theme developed by Leonardo da Vinci in the 1480s. The subject matter was later popularized in Florence during the early sixteenth century by Raphael, upon whose works this composition depends. Bugiardini, as a painter of the Florentine High Renaissance, brings to this work his own brand of harmonious classicism, characterized by the pyramidal-shaped composition, idealized faces, and cool resolution of blues and greens. Although Bugiardini trained in the shop of Domenico Ghirlandaio (1449-1494), the monumental proportions of the figures reflect concerns Bugiardini shared with Michelangelo during the first and second decades of the sixteenth century.

Albrecht Dürer, 1471-1528
Holy Family with a Butterfly, c. 1495
Engraving
9⅜ x 7⅜ (23.8 x 18.7)
Carl H. Lieber Memorial Fund 58.4

Dürer is the first artist of genius whose reputation throughout Europe was based on his graphic work. Typical of the printmakers of the first half-century of engraving, Dürer received his initial artistic instruction from a goldsmith (his father), training that laid the groundwork for his mastery of plate engraving. Yet, unlike his contemporaries, there is nothing dry, tentative, or mechanical even in Dürer's earliest engravings, such as the *Holy Family.* In some ways, this print is indebted to the work of Dürer's great predecessor, Martin Schongauer, in its angular cascades of voluminous drapery and wealth of elegant, incidental detail. Dürer, however, even in youth, surpasses Schongauer by rendering in a convincing fashion a loving family, reposing in a garden in the midst of a delightful landscape.

Lucas Cranach the Elder, 1482-1553
Crucifixion, 1532
Oil on panel
30 x 21½ (76 x 55)
Clowes Fund Collection

As a German painter working in Wittenberg during the Reformation, Cranach painted the *Crucifixion* not solely as a devotional image but also as a propaganda piece in support of the Protestant movement. The scene is traditionally divided: the blessed and the repentant thief are at the crucified Christ's right, and the heretics, sinners, and bad thief are on his left. Cranach, however, gives contemporary relevance to the scene by including among the witnesses of Christ's crucifixion specific portraits of renowned political and religious figures of the time. For example, on horseback on the side of the just are John the Steadfast, brother of Frederick the Wise, and Martin Luther. At Christ's left, in the midst of the damned, are portraits of Pope Julius II, representing the Catholic Church; Muley Hassan, leader of the Turks, who were threatening Europe; and Charles V, the Holy Roman Emperor. Cranach repeated the composition on a larger scale in 1533 (Chicago Art Institute). Our panel is authentically monogrammed at the lower left, and, based on the excellent quality of the execution, it appears to be solely by Cranach's hand.

Titian (Tiziano Vecelli), c. 1490-1576
Portrait of a Man, c. 1512
Oil on canvas
23½ x 18½ (59.7 x 47)
Gift in Memory of Booth Tarkington 47.1

Titian was one of the most sought-after portraitists in Italy during the sixteenth century. *Portrait of a Man*, attributed undisputedly to Titian by scholars, demonstrates the artist's masterful capabilities. In the IMA painting, as in portraits made throughout his entire career, he combined a luminescent pictorial technique with a thoughtful study of the sitter's character. Although the work has suffered losses, much of its original quality has been recovered, revealing the striking facility of Titian's hand.

Hans Leonhard Schauffelein, c.1480-c.1538
Portrait of a Man, 1504
Oil on panel
17½ x 12 (44.5 x 30.5)
The Clowes Fund Collection

Schauffelein, the first known student of Albrecht Dürer, shows in this portrait his indebtedness to his master's example. The painting is based on Dürer's *Self-Portrait* of 1493 (Louvre, Paris) and probably was commissioned to commemorate the subject's engagement. As in Dürer's portrait, the young man holds eryngo, a plant that signifies luck in love and impending marriage. The letter "A" embroidered on the man's shirt, once believed to be part of Dürer's signature, probably refers to the name of the man's betrothed. While much of the painting depends upon Dürer's precedent, the style reflects Schauffelein's own exacting descriptive realism, which successfully captures the expression of the sitter.

Pellegrino Tibaldi, 1527-1596
Holy Family with Saint John the Baptist, c. 1553-58
Oil on panel
15 x 9½ (38.1 x 24.2)
Martha Delzell Memorial Fund 66.233

After being taught to paint by his father, Tebaldo Tibaldi, in Puria, Valsolda, Pellegrino Tibaldi spent his early career in Bologna, absorbing the Bolognese Renaissance style of Bagnacavallo (1484-1542). While Pellegrino traveled throughout Italy and lived in Spain for a time during his maturity, he made repeated visits to Bologna in the 1550s and 60s and is considered today a Bolognese painter. However, *Holy Family* reflects more closely the Mannerist style of Rome, rather than that of the painter's native region. The great muscularity and mass of the figures, particularly evident in the right arm of Saint John, reveal Pellegrino's principal Mannerist source in Michelangelo's Roman works. The packed space and distorted drawing create a highly expressive work.

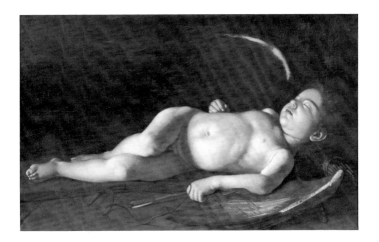

Michelangelo Merisi da Caravaggio, 1571-1610
Sleeping Cupid, c. 1608
Oil on canvas
25¾ x 41½ (65.4 x 104.2)
The Clowes Fund Collection

According to Caravaggio, "To imitate natural things well" was essential to painting. This sense of naturalism manifested itself in his paintings through the use of unidealized types, bathed in a powerful chiaroscuro. *Sleeping Cupid*, far removed from the sweet idealized portrayals of the Renaissance, depicts an unimpassioned view of a child whose profoundly deep sleep suggests death.

When this picture entered the Clowes collection, restoration revealed that overpainting had turned a sleeping Cupid into an image of the Christ Child with his head resting on a cross. Stripped of these alterations, the painting is nearly identical to a canvas by Caravaggio at the Palazzo Pitti, Florence. The Clowes painting is of superior quality, and some scholars consider that this Cupid predates the Pitti version by several years. Technical studies of the painting show numerous pentimenti that are consistent with Caravaggio's works (such as the *Calling of Saint Matthew* and *Martyrdom of Saint Matthew*, c. 1598, San Luigi dei Francesi, Rome), lending support to Walter Friedländer's belief that the IMA painting is an authentic work by Caravaggio.

Peter Paul Rubens, 1577-1640
The Triumphant Entry of Constantine into Rome, c. 1622.
Oil on panel
19 x 25½ (48.3 x 64.1)
The Clowes Fund Collection

The Triumphant Entry of Constantine into Rome is one of a series of oil sketches probably executed in 1622-23 for a set of twelve tapestries that is now in the Philadelphia Museum of Art. This sketch represents the fourth scene in the cycle, the Emperor Constantine returning to Rome after the battle of the Milvian Bridge. With Rubens's typical blend of historical truth and allegory, the narrative is embellished with symbolic figures: Constantine is greeted by the figure of Rome, who presents him with a statue of Victory; Fame blows a pair of trumpets; and Victory crowns Constantine with a laurel wreath. Compositional and figurative allusions to antique art, such as the relief sculpture from the Arch of Constantine and the equestrian statue of Marcus Aurelius, are not only appropriate to the Roman subject, but also reflect Rubens's insistence on references to classical sculpture to aggrandize his painting. Rubens, however, transforms the static nature of the sculptural prototypes into turbulent dynamism through the energetic application of paint and creates one of his fully Baroque works.

Anthony van Dyck, 1599-1641
The Entry of Christ into Jerusalem, c. 1617/18
Oil on canvas
59½ x 90¼ (151.1 x 229.2)
Gift of Mr. and Mrs. Herman C. Krannert 58.3

Van Dyck, a prodigy, executed masterful works as early as 1614. *The Entry of Christ into Jerusalem,* an example of his youthful production, was painted when van Dyck was about eighteen or nineteen and the principal assistant to Rubens. At this early point in his career, van Dyck assimilated Rubens's style, which is evident in the heroic scale of the figures, the vibrant color, and the dynamic composition. The life-size figures convey a sense of immediacy representative of Baroque naturalism, which dramatizes Biblical narratives.

Rembrandt Harmensz van Rijn, 1606-1669
Self-Portrait, c. 1629
Oil on panel
17 x 13 (43.2 x 53)
The Clowes Fund Collection

As a young man, Rembrandt painted numerous studies of facial expressions, and for many of these works he used himself as a model. The Clowes *Self-Portrait* was painted when the artist was about twenty-three and is worked out with Rembrandt's characteristic lighting, dense atmosphere, nearly monochromatic colors, and incisive brushwork delineating individual strands of hair. These studies enabled Rembrandt to create emotionally-charged narratives effectively, with convincing facial expressions that heighten the drama of the scene, and to mirror authentically the extreme states of feeling of the characters portrayed.

Jusepe de Ribera, 1591-1652
A Philosopher (Archimedes ?), 1637
Oil on canvas
49 x 39 (124.5 x 99.1)
The Clowes Fund Collection

The image of the beggar-philosopher surrounded by Caravagges-que lighting is a type that was perfected by Ribera. The asceticism that the philosopher represents, also a characteristic of Ribera's saints, was very popular and suited the more mystical aspect of Spanish Catholicism. This particular work is one of six paintings of philosphers formerly in the collection of the Count of Liechtenstein in Vaduz. The painting is signed and dated 1637 by Ribera and probably was originally intended for a Spanish patron in Naples. While the name of the philosopher is disputed, the identification as Archimedes is plausible because of the attribute of the sheet of geometric drawings that he holds in his hand.

Jusepe de Ribera, 1591-1652
The Drunken Silenus, 1628
Etching
Second state of three
10⅝ x 13¾ (27.0 x 34.7)
Carl H. Lieber Memorial Fund 52.58

An artist who brought earthy realism to all he painted, Ribera here brings the Olympian gods down to earth. His handling of Silenus is perfectly appropriate for the besotted reveler in the train of the wine god, Dionysos. In the early seventeenth century, such debunking of the standard, decorous treatment of the gods was also seen in the works of Caravaggio and Rembrandt. Ribera was only an occasional printmaker; his sixteen etchings all date from his maturity, suggesting that, for him, etching was a diversion and a vehicle for sharing his artistry with a broad audience. Although his most elaborate etchings, such as *The Drunken Silenus*, depend upon paintings, they are far from being reproductions. Each print is a fresh adaptation of the theme.

Rembrandt Harmensz van Rijn, 1606-1669
The Triumph of Mordecai, c. 1641
Etching and drypoint
Unique state
6⅜ x 8½ (17.5 x 21.5)
Mrs. Nicholas H. Noyes Fund 56.161

Mordecai is led through the streets of Susa, honored with the vestments and the horse of the Persian king Ahasuerus, much to the distress of the king's envious minister, Haman, who must proclaim him to the crowd (Esther 6:8-11). As always, Rembrandt brings the touch of humanity to Biblical history. Dogs bark, a baby cries, and each spectator reacts in his own way to the procession. Yet, through Rembrandt's adept use of composition, selective lighting, and emphasis, the crowd does not distract us from the central theme. Only a lifetime of observation could provide an artist with such a rich vocabulary and the ability to use it with such simplicity. Etching for Rembrandt was a natural extension of his sketching. Unlike the elaborate engravings of his time, there is no aversion to an incomplete outline, an omission of a nonessential detail, or the empty whiteness of the paper. By sharing these qualities with his sketches of everyday life, Rembrandt's Biblical etchings reconcile the ancient and the contemporary; the mundane and the sacred. They are thereby rendered timeless.

Pieter Claesz, c. 1600-61
Still Life with Flagon, 1640
Oil on canvas
17½ x 23½ (44.5 x 59.7)
William Ray Adams Memorial Collection 47.2

One of the popular types of still-life paintings in Holland during the late 1500s was the *ontbijtje,* or "breakfast," that often depicted fresh fruit, bread, or cheese. In the 1620s Claesz began to paint breakfasts including objects of everyday life that carried with them mild moralizing overtones. In *Still Life with Flagon,* the smoking paraphernalia refers to the transitory nature of life. The shells, in the lower right-hand corner of the painting, harmonize with the smoking materials; shells, which were desired by collectors, connoted vanity in Dutch emblem books. Paradoxically, Claesz painted the objects in this work with such attentiveness to texture that the appeal to the senses becomes overt and diminishes the effect of the implied moral lesson.

Willem Kalf, 1619-1693
Still Life with Blue Jar, 1669
Oil on canvas
30 ¾ x 26 (78.1 x 66)
Gift of Mrs. James W. Fesler in memory of
Daniel W. and Elizabeth C. Marmon 45.9

The depiction of common objects of everyday life, as seen in Claesz's *Still Life with Flagon*, evolved during the seventeenth century into paintings that ostentatiously displayed exquisite objects. These *pronk* or "fancy" still lifes were brought to consummate refinement by Willem Kalf. *Still Life with Blue Jar* of 1669 is a late work among his mature paintings and is characteristic of the *pronk* still lifes that he had painted since the 1650s. The crumpled oriental carpet, Ming vase, stemware, and peeled citrus arranged in a resolute composition are typical of the successful arrangements of his classical style. The deep rich colors and warm tonalities are subtly applied and enhance the carefully balanced composition. Like Claesz's *Still Life with Flagon*, Kalf's painting incorporates a moral lesson: the open watch on the silver platter represents an admonition to the viewer to enjoy the luxurious objects with temperance, remembering that eternal life is the ultimate reward.

Aelbert Cuyp, 1620-1691
The Valkhof at Nijmegen, c. 1665
Oil on panel
19¼ x 29 (48.9 x 73.7)
Gift in commemoration of the 60th anniversary of the
Art Association of Indianapolis in memory of
Daniel W. and Elizabeth C. Marmon 43.107

The city of Nijmegen is located on the bank of the river Waal in
the eastern Netherlands province of Gelderland. The prominent
tower structure seen in the painting is part of the old fortification
on this site called the Valkhof, an area that marked the location of
a palace constructed by Charlemagne in 777, rebuilt in the imperial Caroligian style by Frederick Barbarossa in 1155, and finally
virtually destroyed during the French Revolution in the late eighteenth century. To the left of the tower is another tower known as
the Belvedere, also part of the old fortifications of the area. The
height of this building was increased during a remodeling of 1646,
and the structure is seen here in its new form.

The Valkhof was a popular setting for seventeenth-century Dutch
landscape painters and was depicted several times by Aelbert
Cuyp, Jan van Goyen, and Salomon van Ruysdael. For Cuyp, the
setting provided an opportunity to convey the golden atmospheric
luminosity for which he is most renowned. The lighting suggests
late afternoon, and the pastoral group in the foreground conveys a
quiet idyllic mood that harmonizes with the nostalgic view of the
medieval structure in the background.

Meindert Hobbema, 1638-1709
The Water Mill (The Trevor Landscape), 1667
Oil on canvas
40¼ x 53 (102.2 x 134.6)
Gift in commemoration of the 60th anniversary of the
Art Association of Indianapolis in memory of
Daniel W. and Elizabeth C. Marmon 43.108

Seventeenth-century Dutch landscape painting often depicts specific, recognizable locations, but Hobbema preferred to compose
scenes with wooded settings uncommon to the terrain of Holland.
The Water Mill, or *The Trevor Landscape,* named after Lord Trevor
who owned the painting in the eighteenth century, depicts the
motif for which Hobbema is best known. He nestles the mill
buildings among clusters of trees, with views of distant fields that
give serenity to the scene. Through his command of color and
lighting—yellow patches of brilliant sunshine interspersed among
areas of cool bluish-green shade—Hobbema creates the kind of
breathtaking landscape that was popular with Dutch urban
dwellers who sought rural places as a respite from their highly
civilized lives.

Claude Lorrain (Claude Gellée), 1600-1682
The Flight into Egypt, c. 1635
Oil on canvas
28 x 38½ (71.1 x 96.5)
The Clowes Fund Collection

Claude Lorrain, although born and schooled in France, resided
most of his life in Italy, where he painted the countryside around
Rome. Unlike Aelbert Cuyp, who in *The Valkhof at Nijmegen*
recorded a particular site, Claude poetically interpreted his settings: locations in the Roman Campagna are idyllized, and rustic
pastoral figures are often added to form tranquil landscapes that
are Arcadian in mood. Although the subject of this work is the
Flight into Egypt, the artist's focus, as in all of his paintings, is not
upon the narrative; the picture is a study of the effect of light and
atmosphere on the landscape. Claude's poetic vision of nature was
highly regarded in the seventeenth century and contributed to the
establishment of landscape painting as a genre equal to the depiction of historical and religious subjects.

Giovanni Francisco Romanelli, c. 1610-1662
The Finding of Moses, c. 1657
Oil on canvas
34 x 45 (86.4 x 114.3)
Gift of the Alliance of the Indianapolis Museum of Art 72.18

Romanelli trained under Domenichino (1581-1641) and assisted the great ceiling painter of the Baroque period, Pietro da Cortona, in the decoration of the *Glorification of the Reign of Urban VIII* at the Palazzo Barberini in Rome (1633-39). Later, Romanelli received numerous commissions in Paris and Rome to decorate large halls in fresco, including several rooms in the Louvre (1655-57). When executing easel paintings, he combined his decorative style with a classical canon. *The Finding of Moses*, probably painted in Paris about 1656, contains classically inspired figures in lyrical and graceful poses. The brilliant color, the most outstanding feature of the work, shows that Romanelli was influenced by such French painters as Eustache Le Sueur (1616/17-1655), who used similar vibrant hues.

Jacques Callot, 1592-1635
The Temptation of Saint Anthony, 1635
Etching
Third state of five
14 x 18¼ (35.6 x 46.3)
James E. Roberts Fund 1984.116

There is an unmistakable theatricality to Callot's interpretation of
the popular theme of the tribulations of Saint Anthony. Callot's
drama is played out under a proscenium arch, with the saint's
island hermitage treated as flats that emerge from the wings. The
dominating presence of the beast hovers above the set like a drop
from the fly rail. Saint Anthony is almost lost in the cast of fan-
tastic demons sent from Hell to tempt him. The theatrical metaphor can be conveniently explained by Callot's lifelong
association with courtly pageants and performances and by his
countless etchings of these entertainments, which were the measure of his fame. Callot's intent in this, his last print, is more
serious. Callot's Latin inscription beneath the image draws clear
parallels between the army of demons released to prey upon the
world and the marshaled forces of men who preyed upon Europe
in an unceasing series of wars of religious persecution. The point-
lessness of war had been the subject of Callot's incomparable series of etchings published two years earlier, *The Miseries and The
Misfortunes of War.* The stage is, therefore, an appropriate venue
for this demonic parody of human self-destructiveness.

Jan de Bisschop called Episcopius, 1628-1671
Fall of the Titans, 1665
Pen, ink, and copper red ink wash over charcoal
on off-white laid paper
11¼ x 15¼ (28.5 x 38.7)
Daniel P. Erwin Fund and James E. Roberts Fund 81.3

Drawing has always been a means to an end – a thought on paper to be worked up later into something more finished. Some drawings, like this one by de Bisschop, are fully satisfying and complete. De Bisschop was highly regarded for his drawings and never became a painter. The inspiration for this work came from a composition by the Italian sixteenth-century master Giulio Romano (1499-1546). It was one of 180 copies of paintings by Italian artists drawn by de Bisschop to introduce the classical Italian tradition into the Netherlands, then dominated by the homebred talents of Rembrandt, Ruisdael, and Cuyp. To propose an Italianate alternative, de Bisschop etched forty of his drawn copies in 1671 as a source book for art students.

Fragment from ecclesiastical vestment, c. 1700
Silk plain weave with silk supplementary warp and metallic
supplementary weft (brocade)
45 x 35 (114 x 89)
Gift of Eliza M. Niblack 30.916

This extraordinary black silk vestment fragment, patterned with
gold, was probably used for mourning. The symbols woven into
this cloth are emblematic of the famous pilgrimage shrine of Santiago de Compostela. The central cartouche with sword and shells
represents the Order of Saint James of the Sword, which protected
pilgrims from Moorish attack. Above and below the cartouche are
the papal tiara and staffs of Pope Urban II, who took control of the
region in the eleventh century. The pilgrim's wide-brimmed hat
and staff, symbols of Saint James, whose legendary tomb was at
Santiago de Compostela, are located to the left and right of the
papal motifs. These symbols are combined dramatically with Baroque scrolling vines and cartouches.

Hyacinthe Rigaud, 1659-1743
Portrait of a Gentleman, c. 1705
Oil on canvas
32 x 25¾ (81.3 x 65.4)
James E. Roberts Fund 56.56

The soft brushwork marks this painting as unquestionably a product of Rigaud's maturity. The style, costume, and wig indicate a date of around 1705, shortly after Rigaud completed his famous portrait of Louis XIV, now in the Louvre. The IMA painting has many of the same qualities of grandeur and presence found in that portrait, but they have fittingly been reduced in this portrait of a lesser personage. This results in a more straightforward likeness. Although Rigaud continued the seventeenth-century use of trappings of rank to indicate social position – the wig, the cloak – he could not resist allowing us a glimpse of the personality of the sitter, for the treatment of the face is surprisingly individual and sympathetic.

Antoine Coypel, 1661-1722
Studies of a Praying Figure
Black, red, and white chalk
8⅛ x 9⅞ (20.6 x 25.1)
James E. Roberts Fund 80.365

Coypel belonged to one of the most illustrious French artistic families of the seventeenth and eighteenth centuries. His father, Noel, was the director of the Académie Royale and his own son, Charles-Antoine, was named First Painter to Louis XV. Of the three, Antoine was the most celebrated. He too was named First Painter in recognition of his contributions to Louis XIV's Palais Royale and Versailles. Besides being noted for his speciality in large mythological and religious paintings, Coypel was recognized as one of the great practitioners of *trois crayon* drawing. This medium, using black, red, and white chalk on a toned paper, was employed to suggest the full range of colors through relatively simple means and laid the groundwork for the growing popularity of pastel drawing in the later eighteenth century. Though this drawing appears to be a close study of the Virgin in lamentation, it cannot be associated with any known painting. The strength of the line, the beauty of the handling, and the straightforward sentiment of expression are characteristics of Coypel's best drawings.

Jean Baptiste Simeon Chardin, 1699-1779
Vegetables for the Soup, c. 1733
Oil on canvas
12¼ x 15⅜ (30.1 x 39.1)
Gift of James E. Roberts 36.22

The subject of this painting, popular in Chardin's day with an ever-increasing number of middle-class Parisian collectors, is known in three other versions (all in private collections). For Chardin at this stage in his career, this type of still life was inspired by similar works of lesser known seventeenth-century Dutch and Flemish artists, like Floris van Schooten, whose names are largely forgotten today by all but specialists. It was only later in his life that Chardin was influenced appreciably by much better known Dutch seventeenth-century still-life artists such as Willem Kalf and Pieter Claesz. Unlike his seventeenth-century sources, however, whose concerns were with describing objects in minute detail, Chardin in *Vegetables for the Soup* summarizes his objects, gently altering their appearances to serve his own pictorial interests and personal sense of color. Through subtle changes in form and texture the picture acquires a poetry that endows the humble repast with a timeless dignity.

François Mondon, 1694-1770
Commode, c. 1744
King wood, tulip wood, marble, and ormolu
34 x 51 x 26½ (86.3 x 29.5 x 67.3)
Gift of the Children of Mr. and Mrs. J. K. Lilly, Jr. 67.10.4

The development of the commode as an eighteenth-century furniture form is typified by the Régence style that continued to be
produced after less conservative designs became popular. As illustrated by this example, the serpentine, or bombé, shape dominates
the outline. Such a form with protuberant front and sides is
known as a *commode en tombeau*. On this piece the geometric
scheme of marquetry combining exotic veneers defines the three
lines of drawers. The top section has a usable center drawer rather
than a fixed panel. Eventually, during the Louis XV period, veneered pieces were decorated with delicate floral designs. The
commode's gilt ormolu mounts and marble top were supplied by
separate guilds; however, the ébéniste, or cabinetmaker, was re-
sponsible for the finished piece and thus "Mondon JME" standing
for *jures-menuisiers-ébénistes*, or "Jury of Joiners and Cabinet-
makers" (indicating guild membership) appears on the top surface
beneath the fitted marble.

Side chair, c. 1710
London
Beech, gesso, and gilt, silk damask
39½ x 23¼ x 25½ (100.5 x 59 x 64.8)
Gift of the Decorative Arts Society of the
Indianapolis Museum of Art 78.110

One of the most important influences on Queen Anne furniture of the early eighteenth century was that of Chinese furniture familiar to the British through the activities of the English East India Company. "India chairs" were mentioned in contemporary inventories, and it is possible that this term denoted chairs such as this one with its highly unconventional design. The most conclusive evidence of Chinese influence is the hammerhead shape appearing at the junction of the front legs and their scroll-shaped brackets. This motif has no counterpart in Western art and is representative of the Chinese scepter head, or *ju-i*. During the eighteenth century, gold leaf was applied to only the most important pieces of furniture. This example is remarkable because it retains much of its original gilding. The backs of the rear legs are plain, an indication that the chair was meant to stand against the wall, a formal concept of room arrangement common in grand interiors of the period.

Giambattista Piranesi, 1720-1778
Carceri V, 1761
Etching
Second edition, first state of two
22⅜ x 16⅜ (56.8 x 41.6)
Carl H. Lieber Memorial Fund 41.26

Trained as an architect and set designer, Piranesi devoted most of his long and prolific career to etching and engraving the archae-ological monuments of ancient Rome, creating works for anti-quarian tastes. What separates Piranesi from other engravers of similar intent was his capacity to invent, elaborate, and manipu-late a view to create an image that was more monumental, more awe-inspiring, and, if anything, more ravaged than the actual site. This satisfied the romantic spirit. Piranesi combined all the ele-ments of his earlier training in the sixteen etchings of the *Carceri.* Though entirely works of Piranesi's imagination, his "prisons" are constructed with such logic that they seem plausible. Vast subter-ranean chambers of Cyclopean masonry rise level upon level to indefinite heights; archways lead to complexes of galleries beyond; huge fragments of ancient sculpture mingle with ma-chines of ominous purpose. Though there are few actual refer-ences to a prison, the pervasive gloom in this labyrinth effectively crushes the spirit.

Antonio Canal, called Canaletto, 1697-1768
Imaginary View of Padua, c. 1741
Etching
Second state of three
11⅞ x 17 (30.1 x 43.2)
Carl H. Lieber Memorial Fund 58.6

Englishmen taking the Grand Tour during the eighteenth century brought home so many of Canaletto's detailed Venetian views that these paintings seemed almost a required souvenir. His etchings, created perhaps in response to the publication of etchings by others after his paintings, present a different Canaletto. As the artist tells us on the title page of his collected thirty-one etched *Vedute* ("Views"), "some of the views are taken of places, others are imaginary." Often the two types are combined. They are tests of Canaletto's powers of invention and of his ability to translate the peculiar quality of northern Italian light into a black and white etching, a particular concern for the painter-turned-printmaker. His secret was to mass short, squiggled, broken lines in the shaded areas and relieve them with broad areas of brilliant white, giving the impression of a landscape shimmering in the heat of an Italian summer. Many painters, once they have established their reputations, turn to printmaking as a means of intensifying their output. Only the rare ones, such as Canaletto, contribute substantially to the art of printmaking.

Johann Joachim Kaendler, 1706-1775
Lovers with a Birdcage, c. 1736-40
Hard paste porcelain
4⅞ (12.5) h.
Gift of Mr. and Mrs. John H. Bookwalter 61.29

This embracing couple, the first of Kaendler's so-called crinoline models, is one of his most successful works, exemplifying as it does his early vigorous style. Because of Kaendler's reference to the production of this model in December 1736, the Museum's example probably dates no earlier than 1737. The strong colors and large expanses of undecorated porcelain are typical of Meissen figure sculpture before about 1745. The theme of lovers is pervasive in eighteenth-century French art, and is often seen in paintings by Watteau, Lancret, and Boucher as well as in prints made after them. However, no design source for this group is known.

Charles-Joseph Natoire, 1700-1777
Boreas and Oreithyia, c. 1740
Black chalk heightened with white on blue paper
12⅜ x 14¾ (31.5 x 37.5)
McKee Fine Arts Purchase Fund 80.365

The eighteenth century in France was one of those rare epochs when all the arts united in a single aesthetic. Under royal patronage and bowing to royal tastes, artists not only painted but also designed porcelain, tapestries, engravings and for the theater. Natoire's *Boreas and Oreithyia* is a quintessential work of that era even though the specific destination is unclear. It is a beautiful rendering of the ancient Greek tale of the abduction of the Athenian maiden by the uncouth wind god, Boreas. The purging of all hints of aggression or crudeness from the drawing conforms to the elevated tastes of the time. Such work, above all else, was to be decorative, and this drawing is related in spirit, if not in fact, to one of Natoire's greatest decorative schemes, the Oval Salon of the Hôtel Soubise in Paris. There, between 1737 and 1739, Natoire painted eight scenes of the love of Cupid and Psyche. The major commission was a temporary victory over his chief rival François Boucher (1703-1770), who received a lesser commission in the Hôtel Soubise.

Frederick Elias Meyer, 1723-1785
The Four Seasons, c. 1744
Hard paste porcelain
9½ (23.5) h.
Bequest of Mr. and Mrs. Herman C. Krannert 75.490-.493

Meyer worked as an assistant modeler at Meissen from 1748 to 1761. At the invitation of Frederick II of Prussia, Meyer moved to Berlin and became one of the most famous modelers of the Royal Prussian Porcelain manufactory. At Meissen the influence of J. J. Kaendler was dominant; however, Meyer produced models of artistic distinction that were especially notable for the elongated proportions of the figures. Allegorical themes such as the Seasons were a popular subject at the Meissen factory and were created by Meyer in 1746-47 and later by Kaendler in the 1760s. The exuberant movement typifies mid-eighteenth-century fashion, especially after the excavations at Pompeii and Herculaneum that inspired the vogue for classical figures.

François Boucher, 1703-1770
Idyllic Landscape with Woman Fishing, 1761
Oil on canvas
19½ x 26 (49.5 x 66)
Gift of Mr. and Mrs. Herman C. Krannert 60.248

France's foremost painter during the age of Madame de Pompadour, Boucher excelled in all subjects he attempted: landscape paintings, portrayals of court ladies, and Olympian goddesses. In characteristic eighteenth-century fashion, he favored rustic scenes enlivened with luxuriant vegetation and picturesque motifs. Whereas nineteenth-century painters aimed at capturing the life and activity of the natural world with penetrating accuracy, Boucher sought to present it in chivalrous disguise, transforming nature into a poetic dream of bucolic yearning.

Idyllic Landscape with Woman Fishing is an invented composition – a blend of observation, memory, and imagination – based on his strolls about the countryside near Beauvais in northern France and stimulated by his recollections of Italy. As the celebrated nineteenth-century critics the Goncourt brothers observed, "Rustic life at his touch became an ingenious romance of nature, an allegory of pleasures and loves, virtues subsisting remote from city and society."

Side table, 1760-65
Pine, gesso, gilt, marble veneer, brass
33 x 60 x 30¼ (83.8 x 152.5 x 76.7)
Gift of Mrs. John H. Bookwalter 78.151

Carved sculptural furniture, which was popular in England from 1720 to 1765, resulted from the influence of Palladian design on such architects as William Kent, who also designed furniture on commission. Marble-topped side tables were often made in suites and were surmounted by matching mirrors; their purpose was purely to decorate or complement the architecture of the room. The naturalistic motifs of this London-made side table are numerous, and the robust execution of the design perfectly embodies the impact of the Rococo style in England. Significant features are the gilt surface of the frame and the beautifully veneered and quartered marble top that is original to the frame.

Pair of side chairs, 1755-65, (one pictured)
London
Mahogany
39½ x 25 x 21 (100.3 x 63.5 x 53.3) each
Gift of the Decorative Arts Society of the Indianapolis Museum of
Art and Lilly Pavilion Discretionary Fund 81.375, 81.376

Chairs of this type were referred to in the 1750s as "ribband-back"
chairs. Such seatwork is characterized by an openwork splat
carved in the form of an interlaced ribbon and represents the English interpretation of the Rococo style. The London cabinetmaker
Thomas Chippendale was certainly not the only individual to
produce ribband-back chairs, but his *Gentleman and Cabinet-
Maker's Director* of 1754 was probably the most influential book
of engraved furniture designs ever produced. Because many craftsmen used Chippendale's designs, furniture such as these London-
made chairs, derived from the *Director*, cannot be said to be by
Chippendale. The chairs nearly duplicate a design from plate XVI
in the 1754 *Director* (plate XV in the 1762 edition). Only the most
skilled carver was capable of translating so literally the intricate
detail from an engraving into three dimensions. Chippendale himself wrote about the chairs of this type, "If I may speak without
vanity, they are the best I have ever seen (or perhaps have ever been
made)."

Woman's apron, c. 1760
Silk plain weave, embroidered with silk and metallic thread
39 x 26 (99 x 66)
Gift of Mr. and Mrs. W. J. Holliday, Sr. 70.46

The complexity of the iconography and its skillful incorporation
into a decorative whole make this apron an exceptional object.
The five decorative columns employ exotic chinoiserie subjects
combined with cartouches filled with depictions of ancient classical myths. Fillings are formed by dramatic floral motifs, birds,
bizarre design elements, and even an opium smoker. A framed
portrait of what may have been the owner occupies the central
panel. The waist pleat marks are still clearly visible on this apron,
which was worn strictly as a fancy dress by a wealthy eighteenth-
century woman. The pleat marks dip in the center indicating that
the apron was worn over the skirt but under the low pointed
bodice. Wealthy aristocratic ladies in the mid-eighteenth century
enjoyed excursions into the country, where they played at being
milkmaids.

Wine glass cooler, 1789
Soft paste porcelain
11¾ (29.8) wide
Mr. and Mrs. Julius F. Pratt Fund 77.51

This wine glass cooler is a well documented piece. Decorated with the *bleu de roi* ground distinctive to Sèvres and marked by the gilder, it also is marked with the date letters "LL" for 1789. In the armorial panel appears the coat of arms of Sir Archibald Hope (1735-1794), ninth baronet of Craighall. The founder of the Hope family is said to have come to England from France with Magdalene, queen of James V of Scotland. Sir Archibald was married for the second time in 1779 to Elizabeth, daughter of John Patown of Inveresic. Originally one of a pair, the wine glass cooler, or *seau crénelé*, may have been commissioned to celebrate their tenth anniversary.

Joshua Reynolds, 1723-1792
Charles Brandling, 1760
Oil on canvas
48½ x 38½ (123.3 x 97.9)
Gift of Mrs. Thomas Chandler Werbe
in memory of her husband 52.34

In Reynolds's account books, he records in the late 1760s the pay-
ment of sixty-three pounds for two portraits of Charles Brandling,
one now at the IMA and the other formerly in the collection of
John Wanamaker. Both paintings, which differ only in the color of
the coats, represent Brandling as the ideal English country gentleman. Charles Brandling (1732-1802) was a man of great distinction: an eminent banker of Newcastle, the High Sheriff of
Northumberland, and a member of Parliament. A leading portraitist in England, Reynolds portrayed Brandling as a self-pos-
sessed individual in a state of repose. The painting is finely executed and is further distinguished by being a rare example of
Anthony van Dyck's influence on Reynolds. The composition
closely depends on van Dyck's *Portrait of Philip, Lord Wharton*
(1632; National Gallery, Washington), which was in the collection
of George Walpole, an acquaintance of Reynolds. In the Brandling
portrait, Reynolds has reversed the figure but borrowed the pose,
setting, and relaxed expression from van Dyck. Reynolds adds his
own sense of elegance to the painting through his fluid application
of paint and creates a beautiful representation of a gentleman.

Francisco José de Goya y Lucientes, 1746-1828
Portrait of Don Felix Colon de Larreategui, 1794
Oil on canvas
43⅝ x 33⅛ (110.8 x 79.1)
Gift of the Krannert Charitable Trust 75.454

As painter to King Charles IV of Spain, Goya often occupied himself with portraits of distinguished officials of the Spanish court. *Portrait of Don Felix Colon de Larreategui* is one such example. A direct descendant of Christopher Columbus, Colon held various military posts, and in 1794 when Goya painted his portrait, he was Lieutenant Colonel of Infantry and First Adjutant of the Regiment in the Royal Spanish Infantry Guards. Colon was also the author of a seven-volume treatise on military justice, which is depicted at the left of the picture. Pinned to his coat is the badge of a Knight Commander of the Order of Santiago. Goya's superior talents as a portraitist are amply demonstrated in this work. To convey the prestige of Colon effectively, Goya chose a lower point of view to elevate the sitter. Colon's head is silhouetted against the dark background, and his expression is reserved and dignified.

William Robertson, active c. 1789
Epergne, 1795-96
Silver
22¾ x 29¼ (57.8 x 74.3)
Gift of the Decorative Arts Society
of the Indianapolis Museum of Art 78.96

Epergnes did not become common in British silver until the 1730s. While some examples were placed on the dinner table, other epergnes such as this could have held a place of honor on the "banqueting table," as it was called – the banquet being a dessert of fruit, wine, sweetmeats, and the like. This Neoclassical epergne by the Edinburgh silversmith William Robertson is unusual for Scottish silver. Even as late as the eighteenth century, large-scale Scottish silver was rare, because Scotland, unlike England, was a relatively poor country and its smiths produced mainly small items such as tankards and spoons.

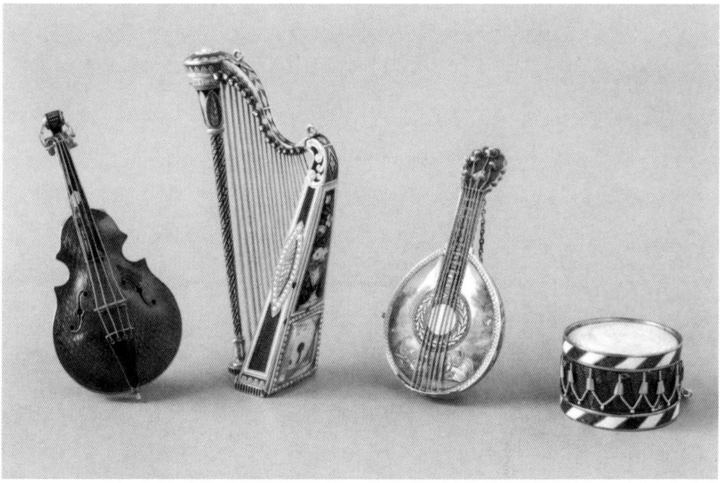

Watch in the form of a violoncello, Vienna, c. 1820-65
Gold, engraved and enameled
3¼ x 1⅜ x ½ (8.3 x 3.3 x 1.3)

Watch with music box in the form of a harp, Switz., c. 1800-50
Gold, enamel, pearls, diamonds
3⅜ x 1 x 1 9/16 (8.4 x 2.6 x 4.0)

Watch in the form of a mandolin, Vienna, c. 1872-1900
Gold, engraved and enameled
2½ x 1¼ x ¼ (5.7 x 2.9 x 0.6)

Watch with vinaigrette in the form of a drum,
Vienna (case), c. 1867-72, Geneva (movement), c. 1775-1800
Gold, engraved and enameled
⅝ x 1⅛ x 1⅛ (1.6 x 2.8 x 2.8)

Gifts of Ruth Allison Lilly
73.70.14, 73.70.84, 73.70.18, 73.70.22 (left to right)

Generations before Fabergé, Viennese jewelers created delicate fantasy watches such as these in the forms of musical instruments. During the nineteenth century it was fashionable to design watch cases in novel shapes that often contained a compartment for vinaigrette, which served as smelling salts, or for a concealed music box, as in this drum and harp. Such watches also were made in the shapes of flowers, fruit, and insects. Their delicate size suggests they were probably worn by women.

Francisco José de Goya y Lucientes, 1746-1828
The Sleep of Reason Produces Monsters
Plate 43 of *Los Caprichos*, 1799
Etching and aquatint
First of twelve published states
8½ x 6 (21.5 x 15.1)
Daniel P. Erwin, Jacob Metzger, Grace Miller Memorial,
Delavan Smith, and James V. Sweetser Funds 62.58

In the eighty etchings of *Los Caprichos,* Goya considered human
absurdities, prejudices, fears, and superstitions. He broadly exam-
ined the skewed logic of the subconscious that often compels
human beings to irrational behavior. Each print, as an independent, personal observation of an aspect of this phenomenon, is
reduced to its essential players and is described by an equally terse
legend beneath. In its scope and psychological penetration, *Los
Caprichos* is unique in the popular eighteenth-century genre of
the artistic "caprice." *The Sleep of Reason Produces Monsters* is
the keystone of the entire series. The artist sleeps at his drawing
table, and his unfettered imagination conjures up a nightmarish
vision of nocturnal creatures emerging from the gloom. As Goya
explained, "Imagination, deserted by reason, begets impossible
dreams. United with reason, she is the mother of all arts, and the
source of all their wonders."

Honoré Daumier, 1808-1879
Le Ventre Legislatif (In the Belly of the Legislature), 1834
Lithograph
13⅝ x 20⅛ (34.5 x 52.3)
Carl H. Lieber Memorial Fund 53.32

Daumier was not only the chronicler of French life, but also the first artist to truly exploit the potential of the recent invention of lithography to produce prints directly from drawings. Nearly 4000 Daumier lithographs appeared in the popular press between 1830 and 1870. The spate of satirical journals, born with the relaxation of censorship laws in 1830 under the constitutional monarchy of Louis-Phillipe, demanded images and provided immediate employment for Daumier, who combined an aptitude for lithography with a brilliance for caricature. *Le Ventre Legislatif* established his early popularity. In a typically French play on words, Daumier not only takes us into the belly of the legislative chamber, but also makes unflattering reference to the corpulence of the bourgeois deputies. Every deputy, though exaggerated into a caricature, would have been immediately recognizable. For his own use, Daumier fashioned a clay bust of each deputy to serve as his model, and in this lithograph he combined them into his rogues' gallery.

Jean-Joseph-Xavier Bidauld, 1758-1846
Parc de la Mortefontaine, 1806
Oil on canvas
34½ x 50½ (87.6 x 128.3)
Gift of the Honorable Paul H. Buchanan, Jr., Dr. and Mrs. Robert
W. Greenleaf, The Alliance of the Indianapolis Museum of Art,
Alicia Ballard Fine Arts Purchase Fund,
and the Allen Whitehill Clowes Fund 1985.189

One of the most celebrated landscape painters of Napoleon's reign,
Bidauld was a native of the Gallo-Roman town of Carpentras. In
1783 he arrived in Paris and studied with Joseph Vernet
(1714-1789). From 1785 to 1790 he lived in Italy, where he developed a personal vision of landscape painting in which he ordered sensitive observations of nature according to the principles
of classical composition. A mastery of cool light and the subtle
massing of tones mark his work, as well as an ability to hold all
elements of his composition in perfect equilibrium. Calm, lyrical,
and elegant, *Le parc de Mortefontaine* represents Bidauld at his
best. The pleasure boat upon still waters, the park strollers and
gliding swans, fuse into an idyllic vision that belongs to the long-
standing European tradition of classicism: civilized man and sympathetic nature achieve a felicitous harmony. The site of this
painting is an estate near Paris that was the property of Napoleon's
brother Joseph. Joseph is thought to have commissioned this work
and brought it with him to America, where he emigrated after the
fall of Napoleon's Empire.

Joseph Mallord William Turner, 1775-1851
*East Cowes Castle, the Seat of J. Nash, Esq.:
The Regatta Beating to Windward*, 1828
Oil on canvas
36¼ x 48 in (90.2 x 120.7)
Gift of Mr. and Mrs. Nicholas Noyes 71.32

When this painting was exhibited in London at the Royal Academy in May 1828, *The Morning Herald* commented that the yachts were "over-masted and represented as carrying sail such as no vessels of their dimensions could carry in such a wind for a single moment." Turner was immune to such criticism. If it had been his wish to accurately record the second annual Royal Yacht Club Regatta held off the Isle of Wight in the summer of 1827, he could have done so. He had made seventy pencil drawings and eight oil sketches of the event from his vantage points aboard a man-o-war moored in the Channel and from the Cowes home of John Nash, who commissioned the painting. Turner did not wish to record a mere race, but to commemorate the pageant of sail challenging wind and sea. For such a larger issue, Turner did not rely on any single sketch, but on a conflation of many sketches and memories, and the result is grander than life.

Joseph Mallord William Turner, 1775-1851
Borthwick Castle, 1818
Watercolor on white wove paper
6⅜ x 9½ (16.2 x 24.3)
Gift in Memory of Dr. and Mrs. Hugo O. Pantzer
by their children 72.182

Watercolor landscapes were Turner's first and, perhaps, foremost achievement, and they provided a steady income throughout his sixty-year career. Turner produced more than 1500 finished watercolors, totally independent of his work in oils. Nearly half of these were commissioned views, destined to be engraved in the vast array of illustrated books aimed at the English armchair traveler or antiquarian. *Borthwick Castle* was commissioned in 1818 for Sir Walter Scott's *Provincial Antiquities and Picturesque Scenery of Scotland* and engraved the following year. Then at the peak of his powers and popularity, Turner participated in the enterprise by the publisher's demand over Scott's objections. Turner's genius in this artistic genre was his ability to take a rough pencil sketch made on the spot and in his London studio work it into a total environment in watercolor. Turner energizes his environment with the powers of nature. Borthwick Castle is rendered as an abiding presence in a landscape that is as ancient as time, but transitory as a gust of wind preceding a storm.

Jean François Millet, 1814-1875
Peasant with a Wheelbarrow, 1848-52
Oil on canvas
14⅞ x 17⅞ (37.8 x 45.4)
James E. Roberts Fund, and Gift of the Alumni Association
of the John Herron Art School 49.48

While small paintings like *Peasant with a Wheelbarrow* reveal
the more poetic side of Millet, this rather intimate picture is actually a transition to the epic canvases he executed for the Salon in
the 1850s. The Revolution of 1848 elevated Millet and the Barbizon
School, of which he was a member, to a new prominence. The
artists of this school devoted themselves mainly to landscapes and
scenes of peasant life in the vicinity of the village of Barbizon in
the Forest of Fontainebleau. They worked directly from nature and
were the precursors of the Impressionists. Millet's typically Barbizon subject, as treated in *Peasant with a Wheelbarrow*, was inher-
ently radical in its social implications since it accorded a rural
genre scene the same significance as a history painting. The picture was begun in 1848 but not finished until 1852, when Millet's
agent thought he had found a buyer for it. From the classical
tradition Millet learned how to idealize his figures, and the peasant pushing his cart becomes a timeless symbol of a rapidly disap-
pearing rural way of life.

Jean-Baptiste Carpeaux, 1827-1875
Une Negresse, 1868
Bronze
22⅜ (56.8) h.
Martha Delzell Memorial Fund 80.202

In conflict with the cold atmosphere and rigid requirements of the French Academy, Carpeaux sought inspiration in the work of Michelangelo, whose power and energy influenced him. This bronze bust recapitulates the theme of enslavement so eloquently explored by Michelangelo and embodies the qualities Carpeaux admired most – action, energy, and twisting movement.

This bust was conceived as a preparatory study for Carpeaux's second major commission from the city of Paris, a monument for the grounds of the Observatory. In the final version of what is today known as the Fountain of Luxembourg, four monumental standing female figures representing the four Continents hold up an open celestial globe, with the black woman representing Africa. Critics highly praised this work, admiring the accuracy of the ethnic features and the nobility of the concept in which oppression and rebellion are effectively realized. In Theophile Gautier's words, "the negress . . . lifts to the sky the only liberty that the slave has, the look, a look of despair and silent reproach, a vain appeal to justice, a bitter protest against the crushing weight of destiny."

Albert-Ernest Carrier-Belleuse, 1824-1887
Ceres, 1877
Terra cotta
32⅛ (81.4) h.
James E. Roberts Fund 81.7

Called a "sculpture machine" by an admiring contemporary, Carrier-Belleuse was praised for his productivity as well as for his verve and imagination. Unlike most sculptors of his generation, who were trained in an orthodox Neoclassical tradition at the École des Beaux-Arts, the young Carrier-Belleuse learned his art in schools that emphasized the decorative arts through apprenticeships and work in the studios of metalworkers, goldsmiths, and manufacturers of faïence and porcelain. Breaking away from the idealizing constraints of Neoclassicism and turning for inspiration to the masters of the eighteenth century, he infused his many fanciful busts and portraits of women with a decorative sensuality and animated realism.

In characteristic fashion, the enterprising Carrier-Belleuse reworked or repeated subjects in cast terra cotta, producing limited editions for the marketplace. While the basic image was cast from a press mold, the surface of each piece, still damp and pliant, was worked with hand tools to give it an individual finish.

Camille Pissarro, 1830-1903
The Banks of the Oise near Pontoise, 1873
Oil on canvas
15 x 22¾ (38.1 x 57.8)
James E. Roberts Fund 40.252

Pissarro's rural landscape was painted at the dawn of the Impressionist era, and its silver light and vast expanse of sky embody the movement's controversial new commitment to recording atmospheric conditions and their effect on the perception of color. Pissarro and his friends, Claude Monet, Pierre Renoir, and Alfred Sisley, left their studios and mounted easels outdoors in order to observe and transcribe nature more directly. This canvas, dated 1873, was painted soon after Pissarro's return from London, where he had fled during the Franco-Prussian war. Pissarro eliminated the more somber earth tones of his pre-Impressionist works and painted this landscape in gently luminous hues. While his loose Impressionist brushwork creates a sensuous surface texture, the canvas's underlying structure locks road, river, sky, and field into the firm compositional network that is a hallmark of Pissarro's style. Unobtrusively tucked into Pissarro's scene are a barge, factory, smokestack, and railroad – clear signs of the growing industrialization that the Romantics and most other Impressionists preferred to omit from their views of the French countryside.

Claude Monet, 1840-1926
Charing Cross Bridge, c. 1900
Oil on canvas
26 x 36 (66.0 x 91.4)
Gift of Several Friends of the Museum 65.15

When Monet produced this canvas in 1900, the Impressionist movement was more than twenty-five years old, and the themes and mood of Monet's aesthetic had manifested some subtle but distinct changes. During the 1890s he turned increasingly from bustling urban subjects or landscapes with figures to remote, silent scenes, where no human presence intruded upon the elements of nature. Like Whistler in the early 1870s, Monet was fascinated by London's vaporous mists and tones, and he spent the winters of 1899, 1900, and 1901 painting more than one-hundred views of the Thames, silent under mantles of fog. As in the earlier series of haystacks and cathedrals, he used numerous canvases to differentiate the fugitive effects of changing light and climate. From his vantage point on the fifth-floor balcony of the Savoy Hotel, Monet dissolved the familiar architectural volumes of Parliament and Charing Cross Bridge into shifting veils of blue, rose, and violet. His three-dimensional subject now floats upon the canvas's rich surface layer, where the artist has dragged his brush in graceful, almost playful curls across the shimmering British haze.

Paul Gauguin, 1848-1903
Landscape near Arles, 1888
Oil on canvas
36 x 28½ (91.4 x 72.4)
Gift in memory of William Ray Adams 44.10

Landscape near Arles was painted during the two months Gauguin spent in Provence with Vincent van Gogh at the end of 1888. Gauguin had reacted against Impressionism's acceptance of the visible world, and he freely altered nature's shapes and colors, often to suggest other layers of meaning or expression. In this firmly composed landscape, however, Gauguin seems most occupied with aesthetic issues of form and structure. The agrarian subject and acid hues show the influence of van Gogh, but this isolated scene of southern France is more directly indebted to Provence's greatest painter, Paul Cézanne. Gauguin greatly admired the elder artist's work, and in this canvas he echoed Cézanne's emphasis on pure geometric forms and their relationship in the landscape. By locking the neat, precise shapes of grain stack and farm buildings into a tight network of carefully arranged brush strokes, Gauguin re-ordered this view of the French countryside to create a timeless environment in which nature conforms to a strict structural regimen.

Vincent van Gogh, 1853-1890
Landscape at Saint-Rémy (Enclosed Field with Peasant), 1889
Oil on canvas
29 x 36¼ (73.5 x 92.0)
Gift of Mrs. James W. Fesler in memory of
Daniel W. and Elizabeth C. Marmon 44.74

Van Gogh usually found his subjects in the direct observation of people, places, and things; but it was his spirituality and intense identification with the forces of nature and emotion that transformed them into powerful personal expressions. This canvas was painted while van Gogh lived at the Saint-Paul asylum in the Provençal town of Saint-Rémy, recuperating from a nervous breakdown suffered on Christmas Eve, 1888, during Gauguin's fateful visit. *Landscape at Saint-Rémy* is the most topographically accurate of four views of a walled wheat field, all executed in the autumn of 1889. Visual tokens of the artist's pantheistic beliefs, the ploughed terrain and rugged mountain peaks seem to pulsate with a fertile inner life, charged by the picture's dynamic brushwork, rich surface texture, and varied colors. Van Gogh described this painting as a pendant to a landscape entitled *The Reaper* (Rijksmuseum Vincent van Gogh, Amsterdam), specifying that the blue-violet tints of the IMA canvas were the chromatic complement to *The Reaper*'s predominantly yellow hues. The paintings also illustrate different stages in the cycles of nature and human activity that inspired van Gogh's life and work.

Georges Seurat, 1859-1891
The Channel of Gravelines, Petit Fort Philippe, 1890
Oil on canvas
28⅞ x 36½ (73.4 x 92.7)
Gift of Mrs. James W. Fesler in memory of
Daniel W. and Elizabeth C. Marmon 45.195

The Neo-Impressionist movement was born in the mid-1880s, when Georges Seurat turned to recent discoveries in optics and color behavior as the basis for his startling new methods. Seeking to "reform" the more spontaneous, intuitive approach of the Impressionists, Seurat and his followers built firmly-structured compositions based on the systematic application of dots of pure color. Hues were selected according to specific laws of chromatic harmony in order to create the most luminous effects. *The Channel of Gravelines, Petit Fort Philippe* is among Seurat's final canvases – one of four seascapes painted on the English Channel coast during the last summer of his brief life. The soft light of the Normandy sun is rendered even more radiant by the dark, painted border that surrounds the canvas. While Seurat's motif is closely based on an actual site, he has accentuated its vertical and horizontal elements, constructing a delicate equilibrium animated by the sweeping curve of the wharf. Even the most thorough analysis of Seurat's theories and methods, however, does not explain the poetic quality that pervades the limpid atmosphere and intricate construction of his tranquil harbor scene.

Paul Cézanne, 1839-1906
House in Provence, c. 1885
Oil on canvas
25½ x 32 (64.8 x 81.3)
Gift of Mrs. James W. Fesler in memory of
Daniel W. and Elizabeth C. Marmon 45.194

House in Provence is a classic example of Cézanne's mature style. Its setting is one of the artist's favorite motifs, the rocky elevation of Mont Sainte-Victoire near his native city of Aix. Though the young Cézanne was a protégé of Camille Pissarro, he did not share the Impressionists' fascination with the changing conditions of the landscape. Cézanne sought instead the essential structure underlying nature, distilling his compositions into carefully orchestrated networks of geometric form. He converted this rugged Provençal terrain into a series of horizontal bands, punctuated by strategically placed vertical accents and the cubic form of the farmhouse. The result is an image that echoes the strength and timelessness of Cézanne's mountain and creates a subtle tension between the two-dimensional canvas and the three dimensions of his subject matter. Building upon his analytic approach, the Cubist painters of the next generation would readdress Cézanne's exploration of the intricate relationships of forms in space.

Maximilien Luce, 1858-1941
La Rue Mouffetard, 1889-90
Oil on canvas
31⅝ x 25³⁄₁₆ (80.3 x 64.0)
The Holliday Collection 79.311

Luce painted views of Paris throughout his career, but this Left Bank market scene offers one of his purest examples of Neo-Impressionism. In accordance with Seurat's application of color theory, yellow and rose predominate in the façades bathed in sunshine, while in the shaded zones Luce's characteristic purple and blue hues prevail. The sturdy rows of buildings lock into the canvas's vertical format, satisfying the Neo-Impressionist call for firm compositions. Luce's pointillist brushwork is surprisingly varied, as small dots of differing size, shape, and direction add to the animation of the bustling scene. His choice of subject suits the Neo-Impressionists' interest in contemporary urban life and his own deep concern for the working man. The rue Mouffetard is a busy artery of a working-class neighborhood, located, as the large sign suggests, near the Panthéon. In the same district were the offices of *La Révolte*, the Anarchist publication to which Luce, an Anarchist sympathizer, contributed illustrations. Luce's Parisian street is little changed today; it remains a popular market district, offering many of the same views and products as those he recorded a century ago.

Edouard Vuillard, 1868-1940
The Seamstress, 1893
Oil on composition board
11½ x 10¼ (29.2 x 26.0)
Gift of Blanche Stillson in memory of
Caroline Marmon Fesler 69.68

In 1889 Vuillard joined a group of progressive fellow students at the Académie Julian in forming the Nabis, an artistic fraternity inspired by Gauguin and the Symbolist writing of Mallarmé and Maeterlinck. For the Nabis, who took their name from the Hebrew word for prophet, the decorative and abstract aspects of form and color took on a new pictorial priority. In *The Seamstress*, scraps of ribbon and lace, chintz draperies, and wallpaper also exist as splashes of pure color and texture that interlock to create a surface pattern as visually engaging as the subject itself. Unpainted areas of the board contribute to the subtle interplay of brown, beige, and red, while the solid pink window is a virtual Vuillard trademark, igniting the entire schema with its brash intensity. The faceless seamstress bending over the cluttered worktable also suits the Nabis' predilection for poetic images of silent, meditative activity, and embodies Vuillard's special gift for capturing the everyday life of the French bourgeoisie. After 1900 Vuillard's paintings became more realistic and less personal, and the intimate scenes of the 1890s are now considered the peak of a career that was to continue for over forty more years.

Henri de Toulouse-Lautrec, 1864-1901
Moulin Rouge-La Goulue, 1891
Color lithograph
66⅜ x 46¾ (168.6 x 118.8)
Gift of the Gamboliers 36.4

Toulouse-Lautrec did not invent the color lithograph picture poster – that had been accomplished by Jules Cheret in the 1860s – but with a single effort in 1891, Toulouse-Lautrec made it an art. In the summer of that year, the proprietor of the Moulin Rouge on Montmartre asked the then unknown artist, who always had a reserved table at the club, to produce an advertisement featuring the nightly performance of "The Glutton" and her dancing partner, "No Bones" Valentin. The poster exemplifies the best of Toulouse-Lautrec's work: a familiar scene, a lively line, simplified shapes like those of his beloved Japanese woodcuts, and a bold color scheme. By October 1891 the poster was hung on the walls of Paris, by January it was reviewed by the press, and Toulouse-Lautrec became a celebrity. Uniquely successful as a poster design, *Moulin Rouge* effectively caught the eye of the beholder, held it long enough to convey the message, and left the indelible impression of a promising good time every night at the Moulin Rouge. In its day the poster was an extraordinary marriage of art and commerce, and it remains the most memorable image of an era.

Hilaire-Germain-Edgar Degas, 1834-1917
Young Woman in Blue
Pastel over charcoal on buff paper
18½ x 12¼ (47.0 x 31.0)
Delavan Smith Fund 38.12

Degas's glimpses of incidental vignettes of Parisian life, such as this unorthodox angle on an impatient saleswoman in a milliner's shop, always give the impression of works rapidly set down on paper. His ability to make something extraordinary out of an ordinary moment has caused him to be aligned with the Impressionists, a group with whom Degas frequently exhibited. But Degas did not subscribe to the Impressionists' pursuit of nature's transitory effects. He wrote, "No art is less spontaneous than mine. What I do is the result of reflection and of the study of the great masters." His use of pastel, in fact, was his attempt to revive a great French art of a century earlier. He carefully posed his subjects, outlined them with an unerring contour, and colored them in such a seemingly effortless fashion that they fully satisfied the modern taste for the personal and the spontaneous. As the German painter Max Liebermann correctly observed in one of the early essays on Degas, "He knows how to compose his pictures in such a way that we do not notice that they are composed at all."

Georges Lacombe, 1868-1916
Vorhor, The Green Wave, c. 1896-97
Egg tempera on canvas
39⅜ x 28⅜ (100.0 x 72.0)
Gift of the Alliance of the Indianapolis Museum of Art 1984.202

With its powerful imagery, striking color scheme, and bold sense of pattern, *Vorhor, The Green Wave* is a vivid expression of the pervasive shift in outlook that changed the art of late nineteenth-century France. Gauguin was one of the most influential painters to insist upon the artist's right to reinterpret nature; and in 1892, when the young Lacombe encountered his followers, he was quickly won over by their independent outlook and decorative style. The setting for Lacombe's seascape is the steep cliffs of Vorhor in the remote French province of Brittany. From 1893 to 1897 Lacombe painted a series of coastal views, and in each composition he was tempted to anthropomorphize the rugged rocks, finding in their chiseled masses, shapes that resembled human forms. He also exaggerated the colors, choosing vivid tints of turquoise, mauve, and gold, and borrowed from Japanese prints the stylized treatment of breaking waves and flattened perspective. Drawn into the narrow gap where the sea pounds the shore, the viewer senses an unsettling air of foreboding, and a mystical element that binds Lacombe and his very individual vision to the larger artistic and literary movement known as Symbolism.

Odilon Redon, 1840-1916
The Yellow Sail, c. 1905
Pastel on paper
23 x 18½ (58.4 x 47.0)
The Lockton Collection 70.78

Redon was the most original of the Symbolists, the late nine-teenth-century artists who preferred to create images that suggested mental states or spiritual realms rather than imitations of the visible world. *The Yellow Sail* is the finest in a series of pictures of women in boats produced late in his career, when Redon turned to a greater use of color. It may represent the theme of the final journey of the soul – symbolized by the gems – across the divide between life and death, in waters that could signify the River Styx. The elemental shapes, flattened perspective, and un-usual colors further remove the scene from the everyday world. The two women are psychological presences who attend the soul as guardian figures, conforming to Carl Jung's concept of the an-ima. As such, *The Yellow Sail* is among Redon's most profound works. It is no accident that during this same period Josef Breuer and Sigmund Freud were undertaking the analysis of dreams, which provided the foundations of modern psychology.

Pablo Picasso, 1881-1973
Ma Jolie, 1914
Oil on canvas
20 x 28 (50.8 x 71.1)
Estate of Mrs. James W. Fesler 61.36

After Picasso created his first Cubist collages, he returned to the traditional medium of oil. *Ma Jolie* is a translation of the collage syntax into the oil medium and explores the possibility of achieving a wider range of textural effects through the use of the illusionistic potential of paint. By using paint instead of ready-made objects, paper, and sand, materials that Picasso often used for collages, he was able to raise profound questions about the nature of painting. Paint can be replaced by the most ordinary materials and yet can imitate any number of these common items.

Ma Jolie, the title of a popular French song and nickname of Eva (Marcelle Humbert), Picasso's lover in 1914, depicts a table with bottles, musical instruments, the score of a song, a newspaper, a violin, and a clarinet or oboe. Objects and words are fragmentary; the dissociation of formal elements creates a new notational system for three-dimensional objects depicted on a flat surface and forces the viewer to synthesize the forms or letter fragments in the mind.

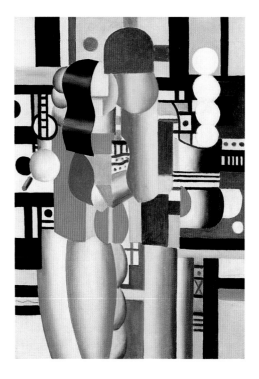

Fernand Leger, 1881-1955
Man and Woman, 1921
Oil on canvas
36¼ x 25½ (92.1 x 64.8)
Martha Delzell Memorial Fund 52.28

Leger, one of the major figures in the development of Cubism, spent his lifetime applying cubist forms to machine iconography. In *Man and Woman*, two robotlike, cylindrical figures are juxtaposed with similar forms that refer to an industrial landscape. The figures are depersonalized and emotionally neutral, and yet their sexual identities are communicated through geometric signifiers (the abstract patterning of their hair, curvilinear forms for the female, and straight, vertical forms for the male). A recurring theme in Leger's works is the human struggle to maintain individual identity in an increasingly depersonalized environment. Flat, bright tones and smooth, impersonal brushwork suggest techniques of mass production. As the eye traverses the canvas, fragments of figures and industrial objects create rapid visual shifts that suggest the increasingly complex sensory impressions of the machine age.

Karl Schmidt-Rottluff, 1884-1976
Mutter (Mother), 1917
Wood-block print
24½ x 20¼ (62.3 x 51.2)
Carl H. Lieber Memorial Fund 57.95

At the turn of the century many young German artists rebelled against the tradition-bound teachings of the official art academies. The established manner was inadequate to express their feelings toward a complex age. The most radical of the young artists, Schmidt-Rottluff, Kirchner, Heckel, and Bleyl banded together in Dresden in 1905 as Die Brücke ("the Bridge"), symbolic of their liberation from the past and their passing over to a new world. Their inspiration came from the arts of societies untainted by industrialized Western civilization–Oceania, Africa, and medieval Germany. The wood-block print became the Die Brücke art form *par excellence*. Not only did the powerful black-and-white, rugged, and brutal images run counter to every established concept of beauty, but the medium itself was descended from one of the most primitive art forms, wood carving.

Amedeo Modigliani, 1884-1920
The Boy, 1919
Oil on canvas
36¼ x 23¾ (92.1 x 60.3)
Gift of Mrs. Julian Bobbs in memory of William Ray Adams 46.22

Modigliani's passion for the human face and figure is evident in all of his paintings and sculptures. As a portraitist in Paris beginning in 1906, he captured on canvas the personalities of many famous artists and writers including Picasso, Max Jacob, and Jean Cocteau. His elegant personal style is characterized by elongated forms that present the subtle character traits and eccentricities of his famous sitters.

The Boy was probably painted during a trip to Cagnes (near Nice). The anonymous subject, who appears in at least one other painting, is not a typical Modigliani character rendering but a study of a figure in an interior corner space. It is similar in pose, delimitation of space, and geometric reduction of form to many of Cézanne's figure studies from the early twentieth century. The influence of Cézanne can also be seen in the distortion of form and scale for aesthetic purposes. The masklike face and blank eyes are a two-dimensional translation of forms seen in the sculptures of Modigliani's mentor, Brancusi, and ultimately derive from African and Archaic Greek sources.

Balthus (Balthasar Klossowski de Rola), b. 1908
Le Bouquet de Roses sur la Fenêtre, 1958
Casein on canvas
52¾ x 51½ (134.0 x 130.8)
Gift of Joseph Cantor 70.85

Born in Paris, Balthus, the second son of a family of German intellectuals of Polish descent, is known for his depictions of young girls and for his landscapes. Self-educated through his study of paintings in the Louvre and in Italy, Balthus developed a style that drew on both the classic formal order of Renaissance artists like Piero della Francesca and on his interest in the Freudian theories of dreams and sexuality. In the IMA landscape the geometric patterns of sunlight and shadow falling on the fields framed by the open window and the dreamlike stillness of the scene reflect these concerns.

Between 1953 and 1961 Balthus lived at Château de Chassy in Morran, a mountainous region in the Nièvre, a department in central France. Of the sixty or so paintings done at Chteau de Chassy, twenty were landscape views from various windows of the château. *Le Bouquet de Roses sur la Fenêtre* is a scene from a window in the north tower that overlooks a field of apple trees. A similar painting without the window frame and roses, *Grand Paysage aux arbres* (1955), belongs to Henriette Games of Paris.

Mimmo Palladino, b. 1948
La Tempesta, 1983
Oil on canvas
84 x 108 (213.3 x 274.3)
Henry F. and Katherine DeBoest Memorial Fund 1986.1

Paladino is one of four Italian artists who were a major force in the "return to painting" movement that developed in the late seventies in reaction to conceptual art. (The others were Sandro Chia, Enzo Cucchi, and Francesco Clemente.) Opposed to the excessive intellectual and political basis of conceptual art, the Italians valued intuition, memory, and the subconscious. These artists drew freely on historic styles of the past – from medieval traditions to Cubism.

The Tempest refers to the *Divine Comedy*, the great allegory by Dante Alighieri (1265-1321) but does not illustrate it. Paladino attempted to reach into what he calls the "collective memory of the past" to create an imaginary world of visionary creatures, who live, like the boatman of the river of Memories, Lethe, in the vale between the spiritual and physical world. In Paladino's painting the figures, whose eyes are depicted as holes in the head, confront the viewer like supernatural and eternal messengers sent from another world to speak without words about the meaning of life.

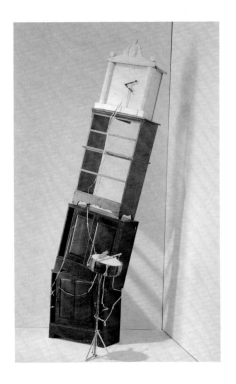

Bill Woodrow, b. 1948
Time and Place for Nothing, 1985
Mixed media, wood and painted steel
72 x 70 x 63 (182.9 x 177.8 x 160.0)
Gift of the Contemporary Art Society 1986.89

Woodrow, educated in London at St. Martin's School of Art, creates tableaux from discarded household objects. In contrast to the assembly-line fabrication of the original object, Woodrow employs simple hand tools, like tin snips and pliers, to impart a personal, handmade look to his work. Woodrow's poetic structures have multiple layers of meaning through association, symbolism, and metaphor.

In *Time and Place for Nothing*, made in the United States during Woodrow's visit to New York in 1985, he wittily creates a "grandfather" clock and a drum from two wooden chests and an early fifties metal kitchen cabinet. While the chests are used "as is," the cabinet has been transformed completely into a clockface and a drum. Woodrow connected the two objects, drum and clockface, with an "umbilical" cord to remind the viewer that both came from the same metal cabinet. One possible interpretation of the tableau is that this work is a comment on the meanings of time. Another view is that the cabinets, empty and barren, suggest the condition of humans in a consumer culture where things are constantly discarded in the quest for the modern life.

American Collection

Mary Wilson
Sampler, 1695 (detail)
Linen plain weave, embroidered with silk
30 x 8 (77.2 x 21)
Roger G. Wolcott Fund 1985.179

The purpose of the sampler, to demonstrate the skill of a young needleworker, is here heightened by the beauty of the designs and the ennobling inscription: "Young Isaac who lift up their eyes and meditate in fields. Young Jacob who the blessings Prizes this woe But Seldom yields. Few Samuels leaving their Players to temple work. Resigned Few do As these in youthful Dayes their Great Creator Mind." Border patterns of vines interspersed with grapes and carnations were originally published in Europe during the sixteenth century in a series of embroidery pattern books; the patterns continued in the folk-art vocabulary through the nineteenth century. In this sampler the patterns, along with the ever-present alphabets and drawn work, are done in various types of counted stitches in colored silk and white linen threads.

Paul Revere II, 1735-1818
Cann, c. 1780-97
Silver
6⅝ (17) h.
Bequest of Eli Lilly 80.186

The Boston patriot Paul Revere is probably best known for his famous midnight ride during which he alerted the colonists of the arriving British. He was, however, a prolific silversmith as well. In the eighteenth century large single-handled cups were referred to as mugs or "canns," to use Revere's spelling. Today the latter term is used only in reference to a pear-shaped vessel with a rounded base and domed, circular foot. This cann, the earliest example of Revere silver in the Museum's collection, is unusual because the owners' full names, "Benjamin and Judith Bussey," are engraved on the side. Bussey (1757-1842) served as a private in the Revolutionary War and married Judith Gay in 1780. The cann was probably among the items that Judith bequeathed to Bussey's granddaughter, Maria Bussey (Davis) Motley. Subsequently, it probably became part of the inheritance of one of Maria's children or grandchildren.

Gilbert Stuart, 1755-1828
Marianne Ashley Walker, 1799
Oil on canvas
29⅛ x 24⅛ (74.0 x 61.3)
Gift of Mrs. Nicholas H. Noyes 52.6

In 1775 the young Gilbert Stuart sailed for London in pursuit of further training, and, after a few lean years, launched a successful career in England and Ireland. He became a protégé of Benjamin West and a likely successor to the English portraitists Gainsborough and Reynolds, but the virtuoso artist was also a *bon vivant* and Stuart was chased back to his homeland in 1793 by a string of bad debts. There he became virtually "court painter" to the Federalist aristocracy of Philadelphia and Washington and created the series of portraits of George Washington that secured Stuart's place in history. This portrait of Marianne Ashley Walker, painted on the occasion of her marriage, exemplifies Stuart's ability to endow his sitters with character and elegance through sheer technical facility. The velvet-draped column and serene pose are stock conventions of Romantic portraiture, but Stuart's particular gifts shine forth from her exquisitely rendered flesh tones and lifelike eyes. Stuart has seized upon the young woman's dignified beauty, drawing her poise and confidence to a pivotal expressive point that stops short of arrogance or disdain.

High chest, c. 1760-80
Walnut
98 x 43¼ x 22¼ (248.6 x 109.7 x 56.5)
Gift of the National Society of the Colonial Dames of America
in the State of Indiana 75.99

This chest is a classic example of the Philadelphia high chest with scroll pediment, flame finials, and shell-carved drawers. The Rococo influence of Thomas Chippendale, which was prevalent in Philadelphia chests, can be noted in the delicately carved and applied decoration of the drawers. Imported mahogany was extremely popular during this period. However, in Philadelphia many fine pieces, such as this one, were still being created of Virginia walnut. An unusual feature of this chest is the unbroken row of narrow drawers at the top, with the shell-carved drawer above rather than in the center of the row. This conservative regularity of the drawers adds to the overall restraint of the design and may well indicate an earlier dating.

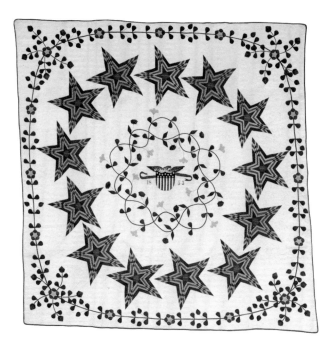

Bed cover (quilt), 1853
Cotton plain weave, pieced, appliquéd,
embroidered with cotton and silk, quilted
88¼ x 87 (224 x 220.5)
Orville A. and Elma D. Wilkinson Fund 75.107

Mid-nineteenth century American appliquéd quilts derived their
designs from a vocabulary of earlier folk patterns. This quilt,
made in the Northeast, is a good example of that continuity. It
combines a basic eighteenth-century composition of a central
form surrounded by folk motifs of vines, flowers, and geometric
stars. The eagle was particulary favored by American folk artists
as a symbol of American independence. The fine quality of this
piece lies in the combination of a dramatic composition with intricately executed needlework patterns.

Dower chest, 1799
Pine, poplar, paint, brass
30 x 51 x 23¼ (76.2 x 129.5 x 59)
Gift of Mr. Edward Huber Dunlap in memory of his wife
Louise Dunlap 78.152

The hinged-lid chest probably from Lancaster County, Pennsylvania is a storage unit found throughout Europe from the fourteenth century to the present. Carved ornamentation was typical of European chests, but rarely used in America, where the arched designs and floral patterns were painted. Several examples, including this one, have survived with the original decoration intact. The primary use of the finely decorated chests, such as those found in Pennsylvania, was storage of linens, so the chests often stood in the principal bedroom. A chest made to order for an unmarried girl was usually filled with linens – the forebear of today's "hope chest." This example has a tulip in a symmetrical Tree of Life design and a heart, a symbol of love. The background is painted in a graining pattern to resemble exotic woods.

Center table, c. 1825
Mahogany, marble, white pine and tulip
30 h., 49 diam. (76.2 h., 124.5 diam.)
Martha Delzell Memorial Fund 79.451

Center tables were used in American parlors of the 1820s and were primarily derived from French Neoclassical models. A notable source for the circulation of fashionable French designs was Pierre La Mésangère's *Meubles et objets de goût* that was published from 1796 to 1830. The four-legged scroll supports of this example illustrate the Restoration style, which was popular in France between 1815 and 1830 and appeared in America in the 1830s. The contrast of well-defined carved elements with simple veneered surfaces marks a sophisticated design typical of the finest Philadelphia workshop. The Winterthur Museum collection includes a table from the same workshop; it is identical in every detail except for a gilt stencil along the top border and the gilt ornament of the legs.

Scroll-back side chair, c. 1810
Mahogany (primary wood)
30 x 49 x 49 (76.2 x 124.5 x 124.5)
Gift of the National Society of the Colonial Dames of America
in the State of Indiana 78.158

During the second decade of the nineteenth century, a number of eagle-back chairs based on the flowing lines of the Greek *klismos* were produced in New York City. As demonstrated in this example, the antique prototype was modified in America: the cresting, or top rail, curves out rather than in, and is contained between the stiles or upright members. The grace and lightness of the original model, however, is maintained. Contemporary sources indicate that side chairs of this type were referred to as "scroll-back" chairs, a reference to the back with its outward-curving cresting rail terminating in round "ears." This example is distinguished by its stay rail, superbly carved in the form of an eagle crouching amidst foliage. In 1792, the Continental Congress adopted the bald eagle as the national emblem. From that time on the eagle became a particularly American symbol and one of the most popular motifs in the decorative arts.

Goddess of Liberty, c. 1870
Copper and zinc
59⅟₁₆ (154.9) h.
Gift of Edward Huber Dunlap in memory of his wife,
Louise Dunlap 81.339

The development of the female figure symbolic of Liberty began with the image of the Indian Princess of the Colonial period and was transformed to Columbia, or the goddess of Liberty, during the early Republic. For ships' masts, signboards, and a variety of weather vanes, Liberty often was depicted wearing the Phrygian cap of freedom and holding a staff with the American flag unfurled. Records indicate that the finest vanes were elaborately finished with gilt and paint. This particular work is illustrated in a sales catalogue of the 1880s from Cushing and White, Waltham, Massachusetts and offered at a price of $150.

Creamer, c. 1897
Clear amber glass
5⅞ (15.1) h.
Bequest of Dr. Ruth Herrick 74.476

In the latter part of the nineteenth century, major centers of glass-ware production shifted from New England to the Midwest. By the 1890s Indiana was the top-ranking state in the country for total glass production. The vast reserves of natural gas in the Midwest contributed to this shift because the intense heat generated by this fuel produced glass with greater clarity and brilliance. The popularity of pressed or molded glass as an inexpensive tableware continued throughout the nineteenth century and spawned the production of novelty shapes and patterns such as the Indian head creamer, designed by Charles Miller, Jr. for the Indiana Tumbler and Goblet Company, Greentown, Indiana.

Asher B. Durand, 1796-1886
Landscape with Covered Wagon, 1847
Oil on canvas
26 x 36⅜ (66.1 x 92.4)
Gift of Mrs. Lydia G. Millard 12.17

Durand began his career as an engraver but took up landscape painting in the mid-1830s under the influence of Thomas Cole. He later succeeded Cole as leader of the Hudson River School, America's first native group of landscape painters. Durand's canvas displays a compositional type favored by Cole in his more allegorical works. Relying also on the English picturesque tradition, Durand divided the scene into two zones. Despite its obvious emphasis on nature, the painting is a metaphor for the young nation – an illustration for the popular theme of immigrants confronting the New World. On the left is the primeval forest, often interpreted as both an untamed realm and a haven for spiritual contemplation by American philosophers and poets such as William Cullen Bryant. The right side reveals the unspoiled wilderness of the new Eden, the proverbial Promised Land, to the pioneers wending their way through the landscape.

Jasper F. Cropsey, 1823-1900
Summer, Lake Ontario, 1857
Oil on canvas
15 x 24 (38.1 x 61)
Gift of Friends of the Museum 71.13

Cropsey, known as "the painter of autumn," was widely acclaimed in his own day for his glowing views of fall foliage on the North American continent. At mid-century he made numerous sketching trips through New England, the Midwest, and Canada, but this radiant vista was actually executed after his move to England in 1856. The British printmaking firm of Gambert and Company commissioned Cropsey to paint views of the exotic American landscape, which were then reproduced as chromolithographs to satisfy the European appetite for glimpses of American scenery. *Summer, Lake Ontario* appeared as the third in the series and was directly inspired by a work of Cropsey's Hudson River School colleague Frederic Church. In spite of its specific title, the canvas is an idealized composition that combines motifs from several different locales. With its setting sun, luminous mists, and tidy farm buildings, the landscape presents a romantic image of man and nature in harmony.

George Cochran Lambdin, 1830-1896
The Consecration - 1861, 1865
Oil on canvas
24 x 18¼ (61.0 x 46.4)
James E. Roberts Fund 71.179

The ideals and emotions aroused by the Civil War inspired a large
body of American genre paintings that were decidedly sentimen-
tal, and the romantic scenario of Lambdin's canvas was well
suited to the contemporary taste for genteel, academic pictures.
The symbolism of the young woman dressed in gray, kissing the
sword of her officer in blue as he answers the call to arms, must
have been obvious to Lambdin's postwar audience. The theme of
the noble departure (and dramatic homecoming) has its roots in
French Neoclassical works of the late eighteenth century.
Lambdin presented his message in the familiar setting of a well-
appointed Yankee library. His lavish attention to the details of
furnishings and flowers reflects Lambdin's dual interest in still
life and genre painting. It was left to newspaper artists and photo-
graphers, such as Mathew Brady, to capture the horror of the war
that marked the end of America's era of untroubled innocence.

Winslow Homer, 1836-1910
The Boat Builders, 1873
Oil on panel
6 x 10¼ (15.2 x 26)
Martha Delzell Memorial Fund 54.10

Homer's legacy of oil paintings, watercolors, and graphics established him as the era's premier interpreter of the American way of life and landscape. He first gained notice as the *Harper's Weekly* artist-correspondent who recorded the less dramatic, day-to-day events of the Civil War. During the early 1870s Homer often explored a single theme through several different media, and this oil painting set on the Gloucester, Massachusetts, coast relates directly to a series of prints and drawings devoted to shipbuilding. One steel engraving from *Harper's Weekly*, October 11, 1873, shows the same two boys within the Gloucester shipyards imitating the workers, thus making explicit what is only implied in the painting by the juxtaposition of the toy model and the schooner on the horizon. *The Boat Builders* pairs Homer's love of outdoor subjects with his fondness for childhood themes, yet the boys' intense concentration and reference to adult pursuits give this small painting a seriousness undispelled by sunny scenes of youth at play. Homer also deftly related the shapes of rocks, hats, sails, and shadows, suggesting a pictorial simplicity that belies the panel's meticulous construction.

George Inness, 1825-1894
The Rainbow, c. 1878-79
Oil on canvas
30¼ x 45¼ (76.8 x 114.9)
Gift of George E. Hume 44.137

The Rainbow belongs to the dramatic series of storm scenes painted by Inness during the late 1870s. Inness matured in the shadow of the Hudson River School, but his response to nature was always more poetic than topographic. He traveled abroad extensively and admired the vision and technique of France's Barbizon painters. A deeply religious man, Inness followed the teachings of the Swedish mystic Emanuel Swedenborg, who theorized that objects in the material world have correspondences in a parallel realm of the spirit. Inness imbued his own landscapes with a sense of divine presence and freely rearranged nature to suggest various moods or states of mind. In *The Rainbow*, he has charged the setting with contrasts of climate, mood, and theme. The passing storm provides sudden atmospheric changes from dark to light, while the ominous black clouds on the left are a foil for the more sanguine symbol of the rainbow. He also juxtaposes the foreground pasture with the view of a distant, unnamed city, creating the kind of individualized portrait of nature that established him as one of America's greatest landscapists.

Theodore Clement Steele, 1847-1926
Pleasant Run, 1885
Oil on canvas
19¼ x 32½ (48.9 x 82.6)
Gift of Carl B. Shafer 58.30.1

For nearly a century, Steele has remained the most celebrated of the Hoosier painters who chose to remain in Indiana. He returned to his native state in 1885 after five productive years of study at the Munich Academy, the preferred school of most Midwestern artists seeking European training. Within months of his arrival, Steele painted this Indianapolis scene, a clear reflection of his Bavarian experience and the beginning of the era of his most distinguished work. The broadly brushed, tonal landscape lies beneath a silvery light that might well have shone upon a stream rippling through a rustic German meadow. During the next ten years, Steele moved "from Munich blackness into the brillancy of light and color of my own climate." In the early 1890s he and Hoosier colleagues William Forsyth, Otto Stark, J. Ottis Adams, and Richard Gruelle began to draw national notice as a regional group that applied the tenets of Impressionism to the landscapes of Indiana, a practice for which they are receiving renewed attention today.

James Abbott McNeill Whistler, 1834-1903
Nocturne: The Thames at Battersea, 1878
Lithotint
Edition of 100
6¾ x 10¼ (17.3 x 26.1)
Gift in memory of Kurt F. Pantzer 80.41

In 1878, Whistler was intrigued by the "nocturne," that metamorphosis by moonlight of even the meanest landscape into poetry. Whistler witnessed this transformation of the warehouses of London's Battersea district into palaces – their chimneys becoming campanili – from his studio across the Thames in Chelsea. To interpret the subtle harmonizing effect of moonlight in oil or watercolor is one thing; to do so in the more restricted media available to the printmaker in the 1870s is quite another, especially since current attitudes suggested that only etching was worthy of artistic interest. Dismissing prevailing practice, Whistler chose lithotint, a little-employed variant of lithography, which itself had been debased by overcommercialization. Whistler recognized the lithotint's capacity to achieve a soft, translucent effect through the overlapping of watercolorlike washes, into which highlights are scraped. *Nocturne* is noteworthy for demonstrating that, regardless of marketability, Whistler would manipulate any means available to a desired effect. Whistler's venturousness placed him in the vanguard of the painter-printmakers of the last half of the nineteenth century on both sides of the Atlantic.

John Singer Sargent, 1856-1925
Rio Dei Mendicanti, Venice
Watercolor on watercolor board
14½ x 20½ (37.0 x 52.0)
Mary Milliken Fund 44.52

For Sargent, with Whistler and Cassatt one of the great triumvirate
of nineteenth-century American expatriates, a vacation diversion
turned into an important aspect of his art. He began producing
watercolors at his leisure in Venice in the mid-1880s, while on
annual winter retreats from his fashionable London portrait studio. Claiming himself no rival to the great Venetian view painters
Canaletto and Guardi, Sargent exclaimed, "I can paint objects, I
can't paint vedutas." Sargent chose instead to record fragments of
Venice: a glimpse down a side canal, a cropped view from beneath
one of Venice's countless bridges, or just the corner of a richly
colored palazzo in the glare of sunlight sketched from canal level.
Hesitating for twenty years to share his watercolors with any but
his closest friends, such as Mrs. Charles Hunter to whom this
watercolor is dedicated, Sargent finally acceded to an exhibition in
1903. Critics and collectors immediately hailed the "snapshot"
quality – perfectly expressed in transparent watercolors – found in
this private facet of Sargent's work.

Tiffany Studios, New York
Pond lily table lamp, c. 1899-1920
Bronze, glass
20¼ h. x 10 diam. (52.7 h x 25.4 diam.)
Gift of Mr. and Mrs. William Ball 75.34

Edison's invention of the electric light bulb in 1879 opened a great range of design possibilities for lighting. The sculptural fantasies created in the early twentieth century displayed originality and movement. Louis Comfort Tiffany (1848-1933) experimented with various types of glass during this period, and his name is often associated with the stained-glass windows and colorful glass lamp shades that were popular in many homes. The style of the pond lily lamp closely resembles international Art Nouveau, with its distinctive linearity and use of plant forms. The bronze base creates the illusion of green lily pads, with stems rising to support delicate trumpet-shaped flowers made iridescent by the effect of favrile glass. In 1902 Tiffany won the Grand Prize for the pond lily design at the Turin Exhibition.

Tiffany Studios, New York
Angel of the Resurrection, 1904
The Benjamin Harrison Memorial Window, (detail)
Glass and lead
348 x 168 (883.9 x 426.7)
Gift of the First Meridian Heights Presbyterian Church,
Indianapolis, Indiana 72.75

Upon the death of her husband in 1901, Mrs. Benjamin Harrison commissioned Louis Comfort Tiffany to create a stained-glass window. The window was dedicated to the late president in 1905 and was installed in the First Meridian Heights Presbyterian Church, where he had served as an elder for more than forty years. Gothic architecture characterizes the church's transept, and these elongated panels of glass convey an upward sweep emphasized by Gabriel's raised hand. The particularly effective use of colors and cased, or superimposed, layers of glass create an illusion of infinite space and luminosity. The window bears the inscription, "Awake Thou That Sleepest. Arise from the Dead and Christ Shall Give Thee Light."

William Merritt Chase, 1849-1916
Dorothy, 1902
Oil on canvas
72 x 36 (182.9 x 91.4)
John Herron Fund 03.4

Among the most memorable canvases by one of America's virtuoso painters are the family portraits of William Merritt Chase.
The versatile artist and influential teacher excelled at Impressionist landscapes and realist still lifes, but the portraits of his
wife and daughters add an engaging personal note to the obvious
evidence of his technical mastery. In *Dorothy*, the artist's young
daughter confronts the viewer with a direct gaze and assumes her
place within a delightful series of female full-length portraits that
Chase painted between 1886 and 1902. With their similar subjects,
subdued color schemes, and unadorned backgrounds, many of
these pictures have been compared to figure studies by J. A. M.
Whistler, with whom Chase enjoyed a brief but stormy friendship
in 1885. The facile brushwork indicates the powerful impact of the
fashionable portrait style of Chase's contemporary, John Singer
Sargent. *Dorothy*, one of several portraits and still lifes by Chase in
the Museum's collection, was purchased in 1903 from an exhibition of contemporary Hoosier art. Chase was born and reared in
central Indiana and continued to participate in local shows long
after his move to New York.

William McGregor Paxton, 1869-1941
Glow of Gold, Gleam of Pearl, 1906
Oil on canvas
76 x 36 (193.0 x 91.4)
Gift of Robert Douglas Hunter 79.345

Boston School painter William Paxton rightly regarded *Glow of Gold, Gleam of Pearl* as the masterpiece of his early career. A transitional work, it predates most of the elegant domestic scenes for which he and his colleagues are best known. In its sinuous silhouette and theatrical pose, the life-sized nude is an unmistakable vestige of Paxton's Parisian training with Jean-Léon Gérôme (1824-1904) and derives from his teacher's academic paintings of women being sold at slave markets. Instead of the smooth finish that lends French nudes their icy perfection and remote idealism, this figure is brushed with a modified Impressionist flourish, and the ruddy reflections of nearby walls give her flesh a sensuous realism, suggesting Paxton's attraction to Impressionism. This blend of contrasting approaches was mirrored in the picture's controversial reception, when it was described as both "entirely modest" and "aggressive nakedness." The critical debate points not only to the problematic role of the nude in the late Victorian era but also to the divided opinions about the academic and Impressionist styles that dominated turn-of-the-century painting.

Frank W. Benson, 1862-1951
Sunlight, 1909
Oil on canvas
32½ x 20 (82.5 x 50.8)
John Herron Fund 11.1

Benson was a key figure in the vital artistic arena of early twentieth-century Boston. After studying at the Boston Museum
School and a Parisian academy, Benson eventually embraced many
of the techniques and goals of French Impressionism. Like his
colleagues Edmund Tarbell and William Paxton, Benson's purest
Impressionist efforts are the canvases of women and children
posed in sun-drenched landscapes. Indeed, the figure of *Sunlight*
has a direct kinship with Claude Monet's women who stride
across the French fields. The model is the artist's daughter Eleanor, who often joined her mother and sisters in posing for Benson's outdoor works. Beneath the dazzling sunshine, Eleanor's
brilliant white form is crisscrossed with the blue shadows typical
of orthodox Impressionism. Even her gesture, hand raised against
the glare, refers to the light that is the painting's true subject.

Edmund Charles Tarbell, 1862-1938
Preparing for the Matinée, 1907
Oil on canvas
45½ x 35½ (115.5 x 90.1)
Gift of Mrs. John G. Rauch, Sr. 82.201

Tarbell was a leading member of the Boston School, which flourished during the early decades of the twentieth century. Like his colleagues Frank Benson and William Paxton, Tarbell painted outdoor scenes with an Impressionist's devotion to sunlight, as well as interior settings that show lavish attention to texture and composition. The works of the Dutch artist Jan Vermeer (1632-1675), rediscovered in the mid-nineteenth century, influenced both the taste and techniques of the Boston painters. In fact, a corner of one of Vermeer's interiors appears in the upper right of Tarbell's canvas. The Boston School painters were renowned for their pictures of beautiful women engaged in domestic activities, and this lady adjusting her hat is typical of their elegant genre scenes. In the hushed stillness and subtle tonalities of *Preparing for the Matinée*, Tarbell's delicate creature seems a willing prisoner in a gilded cage.

Childe Hassam, 1859-1935
Cliff Rock - Appledore, 1903
Oil on canvas
29 x 37 (73.7 x 94.0)
John Herron Fund 07.1

Hassam is arguably the purist exemplar of the American Impressionist movement. Like Benson and Tarbell, he studied in Paris; and from 1886 to 1889 he gained first-hand exposure to the French Impressionist sensibility. After resettling in the heart of New York City, Hassam spent his summers painting out-of-doors along the Atlantic seaboard. Over the course of two decades he returned to the rocky shores of Appledore, one of nine islands comprising the Isles of Shoals off the Maine coast; and this canvas is among his most successful Appledore views. With its broken brushwork, craggy shore, and broad expanse of sea, the painting exudes the same spirit as Monet's marines of Etretat and Belle-Île from the mid-1880s. Hassam displays a confident, free handling, as the rich surface and division of color vary from the loose treatment of the sun-bleached rocks, to the overlapping strokes and vibrant hues of the foreground water, to the more even texture and tone of the distant horizon. While the picture plane does achieve a certain flatness in the background areas, the rock retains its sturdy sense of volume – an emphasis on solidity and realism that characterizes the American brand of Impressionism.

Julian Alden Weir, 1852-1919
Still Life, c. 1902-05
Oil on canvas
24 ¾ x 36 ⅛ (62.9 x 91.8)
James E. Roberts Fund 26.92

Like many of America's leading artists at the turn of the century, Weir was the product of traditional academic training and had wide exposure to French Impressionism. A vital force in several artists' associations, Weir joined such colleagues as Hassam, Benson, and Tarbell in 1897 to form the Ten American Painters, a stylistically diverse organization usually identified with American Impressionism. While landscapes and portraits played the most prominent roles in their repertoires, the still life was also a popular and practical subject. Most of Weir's still lifes were floral pieces, and this ambitious assemblage of fruit, vegetables, and tableware is unique in his oeuvre. With thick strokes of the brush, Weir suggested the textures of porcelain, fabric, and food and created a straightforward composition remarkably close in spirit to the works of nineteenth-century French realist Antoine Vollon.

John Sloan, 1871-1951
Red Kimono on the Roof, 1912
Oil on canvas
24 x 20 (61 x 50.8)
James E. Roberts Fund 54.55

Red Kimono on the Roof is one of Sloan's classic pictures, painted at the height of his career. A Philadelphia newspaper illustrator, Sloan moved to New York in 1904 and joined other journalist colleagues in forming The Eight, an artists' group whose preference for down-to-earth subject matter earned them the epithet of Ash Can School. In the bustling activity of New York's lower East Side, the painters found their slice-of-street-life motifs, which they recorded with broad, vigorous strokes and a conscious avoidance of sentimentality. Even Sloan, an active socialist and the most politically sensitive of the group, refused to let his paintings serve as editorials for his opinions. This unglorified glimpse of a woman, clothespin in mouth, attending to her laundry, may well have been painted from Sloan's studio window, which would explain the elevated vantage point. The picture's sense of immediacy and direct observation is enhanced by the spontaneous brushwork and Sloan's attention to light and shadow.

Maurice Prendergast, 1859-1924
The Park, Salem, c. 1910
Watercolor over pencil on white paper
14 x 19⅞ (35.6 x 50.5)
Gift of the Gamboliers 34.16

Prendergast is unique and independent among American artists.
His study in Paris at the mature age of thirty-one was noninfluen-
tial. His association from 1904 with the New York painters in the
circle of Robert Henri had no impact on his work. While they
depicted the grittier aspects of street life, Prendergast delighted in
the human promenade in the park or at the beach, which he
painted again and again with almost childlike enthusiasm. As a
pure colorist, Prendergast was at his best in transparent watercolor. "Explosions in a color factory" was the apt characterization
of his watercolors by one critic; while another in Boston in 1914
grudgingly admitted: "The exasperating part of it all is that his
style is so suited to the subjects he uses."

Paul Manship, 1885-1966
The Rape of Europa, 1925
Gilt bronze on onyx base
25 X 29 X 8⅞ (63.5 X 73.7 X 22.5)
Gift of Miss Lucy M. Taggart 50.30

With elegant forms and ingenious balance of forces, Manship has achieved one of the wittiest interpretations of the classical myth of Europa. The Phoenician maiden was carried off by the amorous Zeus, who transformed himself into a bull to spirit her across the sea to Crete. Never has there been a more poised victim than Manship's Europa, erect and cross-legged, riding backward as she listens attentively to the whispers of Eros. The artist's life-long appreciation for Archaic Greek sculpture appears in the maiden's hieratic form, the emphasis on profile views, and the stylized treatment of hair and drapery; while the muscular bull shows the influence of ancient Minoan animal forms. Manship's rhythmic composition is an endless pairing of horizontals and verticals, speed and arrested motion, as the bull's horns, tail, and legs flow gracefully against the curving backs of the dolphins, contrasting with Europa's upright posture and the stair-stepped angles of the onyx base. Indulging his interest in the surface properties of bronze, Manship added a gilded finish to this sculpture, which marries levity with sophistication and casts ancient sources in twentieth-century designs.

Sidney Waugh, 1904-1963
Gazelle Bowl, c. 1939
Optical glass
7 x 6½ x 6½ (17.8 x 16.5 x 16.5)
The Carl H. Lieber Memorial Fund 39.11

In 1932 a new formula enabled the Corning Glass Works to produce an extremely pure and highly refractive optical glass. The new crystal known as 10M, was a perfect medium for Steuben's design direction in the 1930s: volumetric shapes equivalent to the streamlined architecture of the period. The *Gazelle Bowl* exemplifies this new aesthetic and was the first engraved piece designed for Steuben by the sculptor Sidney Waugh. It is now considered one of Steuben's classics, having been reproduced more than fifty times since its debut at the Fine Arts Society exhibition in London 1935.

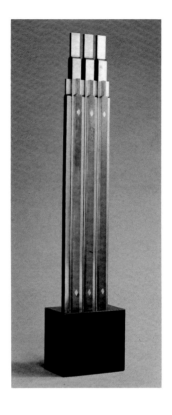

John Storrs, 1885-1956
New York, c. 1925
Brass and steel on black marble base
25⅞ x 5½ x 3½ (65.7 x 14.2 x 8.9)
Discretionary Fund 73.8

The art of John Storrs has a sharp precision and geometric purity that make him an ideal standard-bearer for modernist sculpture of the machine age. A Chicago native who trained in Rodin's Paris studio, Storrs made a decisive stylistic shift around 1917 toward non-objective works and faceted planes inspired by Cubism. In the 1920s he began creating the spare and elegant skyscrapers that are considered his masterpieces. These severe flutes of brass, which Storrs entitled *New York*, can be read as an essay in abstract constructivist form or as a towering miniature building with stepped façades and consciously modern angles. The hardware holding the smooth, cold rods together is concealed by diamond-shaped steel lozenges, appropriate to Storrs's geometric rigor and his penchant for combining different metals in one work of art. A vivid representative of the sleek new giants of the modern urban environment, *New York* also symbolized the artist's belief in the interdependence of sculpture and architecture.

Paul Frankl, 1878-1962
Table, 1928
Glass, steel
24⅜ x 17 x 17 (61.9 x 43.2 x 43.2)
Gift of Mr. and Mrs. Robert H. Morse 71.214.2

Frankl immigrated to the United States from Vienna in 1914. He first gained recognition for his furniture designs at the *Exposition International des Arts Décoratifs* in Paris, 1925. The structural formalism of this small table exemplifies the architectural approach that Frankl used in furnishing interiors. Bookcases, dressing tables, and desks designed by Frankl all display a characteristic interplay of planar forms rather than relying upon surface embellishment. He also experimented with new materials. This table is made of three tiers of glass suspended in a cadmium steel frame. Frankl expressed his conviction about materials in his 1930 book *Form and Re-Form*, stating that "modern science and engineering must be utilized in the artistic language of our own day."

Thomas Hart Benton, 1889-1975
Henry Look Unhitching, c. 1942
Tempera on masonite
23⅛ x 27⅝ (58.8 x 70.2)
Gift of Mr. and Mrs. Joseph Cantor 60.273

During the years between the first and second World Wars, a group of painters known as the Regionalists became prominent for advocating art that represented the American scene. These artists, who included Thomas Hart Benton, Grant Wood, and John Steuart Curry, promoted American idealism and a national aesthetic of realism that was consciously distinct from that of the modern European abstractionists. Benton, the group's leader and impassioned spokesman, created paintings that celebrated American life, particularly in the rural Midwest. His compositions writhe with animation, as in *Henry Look Unhitching*, where the fertile earth and cloud-filled sky are drawn with rhythmic curving lines that suggest the vitality of the forces of nature. The dynamism of the landscape, however, is subdued by the reverie of the stooped farmer, who unhitches his horse after a day's work. The painting is a characteristic example of Benton's spirit and style, which, after an initial ironic flirtation with abstraction prior to 1920, changed little in the course of his long career.

Edward Hopper, 1882-1967
Hotel Lobby, 1943
Oil on canvas
32¼ x 40¾ (81.9 x 103.5)
William Ray Adams Memorial Collection 47.4

In contrast to Benton, whose works were intended to glorify the virtues of American rural life, Hopper is best known for urban scenes infused with the loneliness and banality that are also part of the American experience. Alienation and isolation became persistent themes for Hopper; he often painted solitary figures gazing from windows or isolated persons gathered in public places. *Hotel Lobby* is seen as if by chance, but the encounter is anything but casual–the schema is defined by cold, strict geometry and was carefully orchestrated through four preparatory drawings. The compositional rigor adds a sense of spatial dislocation to the foyer, whose cheerlessness is enhanced by the harsh, raking light and the lack of rapport among the figures. The setting, with its elevated vantage point, is oddly theatrical, and could have been at least partially inspired by Hopper's frequent attendance at Broadway plays, which he preferred to view from the balcony. Although the manner and mood of Hopper's works differed significantly from Benton's, both artists rejected European influences in favor of the pursuit of realism as a national style.

Georgia O'Keeffe, 1887-1986
Pelvis with the Distance, 1943
Oil on canvas
23⅞ x 29¾ (60.6 x 75.6)
Gift of Anne Marmon Greenleaf in memory of
Caroline Marmon Fesler 77.229

In 1929, when O'Keeffe began to spend her summers in New Mexico, she was already an established artist whose powerful images included landscapes and cityscapes as well as magnified views of flowers and shells. Yet the colors, shapes, and vistas of the Southwest rapidly became central to her visual repertoire. In *Pelvis with the Distance* she juxtaposed an enormous skeletal form rising majestically from the flat sandy foreground with a mountain range lying low on the horizon. The radical manipulation of scale and perspective, and the strong but elegant contours of the bone exemplify O'Keeffe's genius for reducing (or magnifying) nature's forms to their abstract essences. Gazing through the bone's aperture to the vibrant desert sky beyond, it is tempting to empathize with O'Keeffe's approach to her "bone series." As she wrote to collector Caroline Marmon Fesler: "It is a kind of thing that I do that makes me feel I am going off into space – in a way that I like – and that frightens me a little because it is so unlike what anyone else is doing –. I always feel that sometime I may fall off the edge – It is something I like so much to do that I dont (sic) care if I do fall off the edge –"

David Smith, 1906-1965
Egyptian Barnyard, 1954
Wrought and soldered silver
14½ x 24 (37.0 x 61.0)
Gift of Mr. and Mrs. J. W. Alsdorf 60.279

Smith was born in Decatur, Indiana, to Harvey Martin Smith, a telephone engineer, and Golda Stoler, a school teacher. In the summer of 1925 he worked in a Studebaker plant in South Bend, an experience that he recalled in later life as important for his realization of the artistic potential of industrial materials. After a semester at Notre Dame University, Smith left for New York to study art. Later, at Bolton Landing in upper New York State, he built his home and studio, "Terminal Iron Works." Although best known for his steel sculptures, Smith employed a variety of metals. Towle Silversmiths commissioned him to make a work in silver for the exhibition "Sculpture in Silver from Islands in Time." To fulfill the commission Smith created *Birthday*, which was completed on his own birthday, March 9, 1954. Eleven days later he finished *Egyptian Barnyard*, a larger work also of silver. Unlike *Birthday*, *Barnyard* is drawn out into fluid lines of metal as if Smith were "drawing" with silver. A flat sheet in the center resembles the outline of an Egyptian mummy, and the overall shape recalls both a landscape and a bird. The multiple and simultaneous readings of forms are typical of Smith's work.

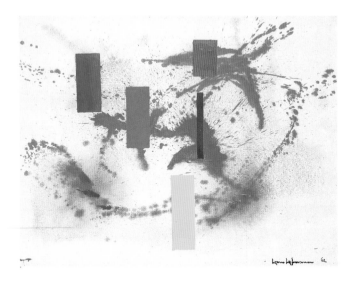

Hans Hofmann, 1880-1966
Poem d'Amour, 1962
Oil on canvas
36¼ x 48 (92.1 x 121.9)
Gift of the Contemporary Art Society 64.15

Hofmann began teaching young American artists in the 1930s, and exerted a broad influence on Abstract Expressionism during its formative years. He encouraged his students to incorporate tendencies of style and feeling previously thought to be contradictory. His art theory included the traditions of Malevich, Kandinsky, Klee, and Mondrian. *Poem d'Amour* synthesizes the formal rationalized approach of Mondrian with the improvisatory and spontaneous qualities of Kandinsky. The duality of the opposing poles of emotion and strict intellectuality are central to Hofmann's teachings and to the painting itself. In *Poem d'Amour* color rectangles create energy and produce simultaneous perceptions of flatness and depth. The surface of the painting is activated without violating the two-dimensionality of the picture plane. The dripped and spattered background has been created through an automatic, Surrealist technique that spontaneously allows forms from the subconscious to emerge.

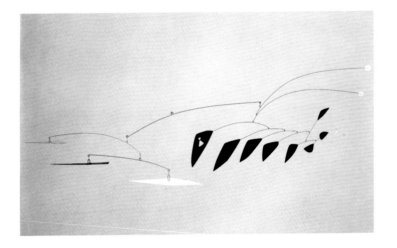

Alexander Calder, 1898-1976
Two White Dots in the Air, 1958
Sheet metal and wire
Length overall 100 (240)
Gift of Joseph Cantor 1987.89

Calder, born to a family of Philadelphia sculptors, is best known today for his invention of a type of moving abstract sculpture, christened by Marcel Duchamp, "mobile." Calder credited his visit to Mondrian's Paris studio in 1930 as the inspiration for the first mobile. Upon seeing colored squares of cardboard (used by Mondrian to plan compositions for his paintings) tacked upon the wall, Calder imagined the rectangles moving. Initially, many of Calder's mobiles were motorized, but he came to prefer air-driven ones like the IMA's because of the element of chance involved in their movement.

Like many mobiles from the 1940s and 50s, *Two White Dots in the Air* combines a series of related organic shapes with geometric shapes. Two spritely white dots springing upward from the more somber black shapes give a light-hearted note to the entire moving creation.

Robert Indiana, b. 1928
LOVE, 1966
Acrylic on canvas
71⅞ x 71⅞ (180.7 x 180.7)
James E. Roberts Fund 67.08

Word images are an important aspect of Robert Indiana's Pop Art work. His typographical designs are intended to give visual potency to imagery that had become commonplace in American culture. By using the aggressive attention-getting devices of billboard design, such as strident color and oversized scale, Indiana incorporated the visual techniques and vocabulary of commerical advertising into the realm of so-called fine art. The *LOVE* series is probably his best-known design. For immediate impact, the stacked block letters are painted in bold, clashing colors with sharp edges. The IMA also has a monumental sculpture of the same design, which has become closely associated with the identity of the Museum.

Richard Anuszkiewicz, b.1930
Red Edged Emerald Green, 1980
Acrylic on canvas
48 x 48 (121.9 x 121.9)
Director's Discretionary Fund 80.195

Rather than treating the canvas in the traditional sense as a "window" through which one views the subject, Anuszkiewicz animates the picture plane by creating optical illusions with an abstract geometric pattern. Op Art, as this type of painting is called, alters the viewer's visual perceptions and explores the kinetic effects of patterns. In *Red Edged Emerald Green* the crisply painted lines of alternating complementary colors that radiate from the central green square appear to vibrate before the viewer. Through the careful control of the basic properties of line, color, and shape, the artist manipulates the way we see, creating illusory perceptions.

Richard Estes, b. 1936
Car Reflections, c. 1968
Acrylic on masonite
48 x 30 (121.0 x 76.2)
Purchased with Funds from the Penrod Society
and the National Endowment for the Arts 71.207

Estes paints the man-made environments of New York City in a photographic style called Superrealism. In this work he depicts the corner of West 20th Street and Fifth Avenue by reproducing the reflected images of two closely parked cars. *Car Reflections* dates from the late 1960s, when Superrealism enjoyed great success. While the painting appears to replicate what the camera sees from a single viewpoint, the artist has selectively synthesized the scene from a number of photographs. By accurately recording the surfaces from these multiple images of the same scene, Estes renders more data than eye and mind can assimilate. The painting is fascinating for the exact rendering of the highly reflective surfaces and the spatially complicated composition in which reality and reflection are intermingled.

Chuck Close, b. 1940
Keith Four Times, 1975
Lithograph
Printer's proof; numbered edition of 50
30 x 80 (76.2 x 203.2)
Roger G. Wolcott Fund 1985.221

The century-old confrontation between painting and photography has, since 1967, been reconciled in the work of Chuck Close. Taking portrait photographs of himself, his family, and his friends, Close superimposes a grid and transfers the image, square by square, to his paper or canvas. Printmaking gives Close a reason to return to drawing, something he finds unnecessary in his painting. *Keith Four Times*, in a sense, examines the evolution of a Close drawing. Beginning with the smallest image composed of simple, clearly defined blots of black on white, he moves through progressive additions and refinements to a work of great tonal variety and remarkable realism. Read in reverse order, these four lithographs on one sheet create a second illusion, that of a photograph seen first up close and then becoming more and more generalized as it recedes into the distance.

George Rickey, b. 1907
Two Lines Oblique Down, Variation III, 1970
Stainless steel
25 ft. high; blades 15 ft. each (7.35 m high; blades 4.41 m each)
The Orville A. and Elma D. Wilkinson Fund 75.178

Kinetic art uses prevailing technology to produce moveable sculpture embodying time and motion. The introduction of the idea of movement in sculpture was first articulated by Boccioni in his *Technical Manifesto of Futurist Sculpture* in 1912. Other important seminal figures in the development of kinetic sculpture were Marcel Duchamp, Naum Gabo, Laszlo Moholy-Nagy, and Alexander Calder. Rickey, like Calder, uses random wind currents to set his sculptures in motion. While Calder's mobiles are biomorphic forms that suggest natural objects, Rickey's linear forms are oscillating, intersecting blades that create geometric shapes, which are more closely related to the early Constructivist origins of kinetic sculpture. In his work Rickey focuses on the organization of movement itself. Form is sublimated, and a specific quality of movement is defined and emphasized. By using ball bearings in the sculpture joints, the geometric elements move in an even, graceful, and controlled passage through space and time. The scale of the sculpture is especially significant in kinetic art because the speed of the pendulum is in reverse proportion to the length; as the scale increases, the time span of the movement is altered.

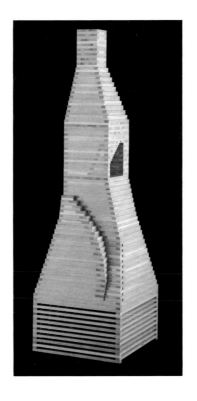

Jackie Ferrara, b. about 1940
A 203 KAHV, 1979
Pine
102 x 31½ x 31½ (259.1 x 80.0 x 80.0) (at base)
Gift of the Contemporary Art Society 80.237

In contemporary art the demarcation between sculpture and ar-chitecture is not always clearly defined, and the constructions of Jackie Ferrara exemplify this ambiguity. *A 203 KAHV,* which re-sembles rising asymmetrical pyramids, is an assemblage of one-by-two-inch pine boards. The form rises and changes at regular intervals, a regularity that is first carefully plotted on graph paper through an elaborate mathematical system of proportion. Into the stepped form Ferrara often injects a small niche or gap that is equally systematic in its proportional design. While Ferrara calls her constructions sculpture, works like *A 203 KAHV* have archi-tectural associations such as Egyptian tombs or pre-Columbian temples. Her work appears visually simple, but it is actually con-structed upon complex geometric principles, an element that fur-ther links her pieces with ancient architecture.

Philip Pearlstein, b. 1924
Nude in Hammock, 1983
Color etching and aquatint
Printer's proof; numbered edition of 50
30¼ x 40⅜ (76.8 x 102.6)
Thomas W. Ayton, Eugene Beesley, Edwin Binney, Helen Adams
Bobbs, and Paul Buchanan Funds 1983.70

After World War II the appearance of European-style print work-shops in America sparked an explosion of creative printmaking. Artists, who might not otherwise have ventured into printmak-ing, were encouraged to do so. They were provided facilities and the technical knowledge of a master printmaker. Undoubtedly, an artist as firmly committed to drawing as Pearlstein would have produced at least simple prints without such encouragement, but the print workshop system has allowed him, since the late 1960s, to experiment with compositions of ever greater complexity and difficulty. *Nude in Hammock* is a case in point. Though it re-prises Pearlstein's familiarly unorthodox angle of a model posed on elaborate studio props, the model is daringly foreshortened and seen through the complicated web of the mesh hammock. The legibility of this tricky scheme demonstrates Pearlstein's growing sophistication as a painter-printmaker.

Asian Collection

Large jar, c. 2500 B.C.
Painted pottery (Banshan type ware)
16¼ x 25⁹⁄₁₆ x 25⁹⁄₁₆ (41.3 x 64.9 x 64.9)
Gift of Mr. and Mrs. Eli Lilly 60.144

This storage jar, from the period of Neolithic prehistory in China, reveals the delight in linear design that was to become a prominent feature throughout the history of art in China. The spiral lines of alternating black and brown are painted with bold brush strokes on the hand-formed, reddish buff earthenware. Many similar pieces, encircled by repetitive patterns, were discovered at the burial ground at Banshan, Gansu Province, and they are typical products of the Yangshao culture, a civilization named after that important Neolithic settlement in Henan Province.

Crested-bird pendant, 13th century B.C.
Shang dynasty
Nephrite
3¾ x 1½ x ⅛ (9.4 x 3.5 x 0.3)
Gift of Mr. and Mrs. Eli Lilly 60.66

The term "jade" is actually used for a wide variety of semiprecious hardstones that have been revered in China since prehistoric times. This fine jade, fashioned as a profile of a bird with double lines creating designs on the body, is quite similar to examples among the 700 jades recently recovered from the tomb of a royal consort in the last capital of the Shang dynasty. It probably served as part of an aristocratic ornament. Unlike people of other civilizations who developed metal technology, the early Chinese rarely used metal for bodily adornments, preferring natural materials, and the veneration they had for jade may well explain why such pendants were among the more popular types of jewelry in ancient China.

Covered wine vessel (*guang*), 13th-12th century B.C.
Shang dynasty
Bronze
8⅜ x 9 x 3 (21.2 x 23 x 7.7)
Gift of Mr. and Mrs. Eli Lilly 60.43

This ceremonial wine vessel with a removable lid demonstrates the complex sculptural qualities so often exhibited in the bronze casting of ancient China. As in many early bronzes, the decor is animated with zoomorphic designs such as birds and dragons, set against a background filled with fine spiral patterns, and the vessel itself is a composite of animal forms. Precious bronze vessels like this were made for the highest levels of aristocracy and were intended solely for sacrificial ceremonies for the ancestors of the ruling elite. On the inside of the cover is an inscription, presumably the name of the clan or the person to whom the vessel is dedicated.

Tripod bowl, (*ding*), 13th-12th century B.C.
Shang dynasty
Bronze
8 x 6 x 6 (20.3 x 15.4 x 15.4)
Gift of Mr. and Mrs. Eli Lilly 60.288

Magnificent bronze vessels have become nearly synonymous with the first historical period in China, the Shang dynasty. From practically the very beginning of the Bronze Age, these exquisite ritual vessels were cast in piece molds with unparalleled technical skill into shapes and designs befitting the importance of their ceremonial role. The *ding*, a bowl with legs to support it over the fire for cooking offerings, was the most revered and important type of ceremonial vessel. Some particularly renowned ones were even considered symbolic of the right to rule. Near the rim on the interior of this *ding*, which has a unique combination of tiger and whorl motifs, is a pictogram of the high-ranking woman to whom the vessel was dedicated.

Jar with lid, 9th-8th century B.C.
Glazed stoneware
2 x 2½ x 2½ (5.1 x 6.5 x 6.5)
Gift of the Alliance of the Indianapolis Museum of Art 1985.3

Recent excavations of similar glazed objects have shown that an early sophisticated tradition of ceramic production existed in southeastern China (from Anhui to Zhejiang). This jar, like some of the others from this area, is small in size, has a rather dramatic profile, appliqué S spirals, a shoulder design of diagonally lined dots within incised bands, and is covered inside and out with a thick green glaze. The southern culture from which the jar came is just beginning to be recognized and understood, and relative dates for the ceramics are still problematical. Yet evidence continues to support the proposed ninth-eighth century B.C. date, which corresponds to the late Western Zhou dynasty of the north.

Bell, 6th century B.C.
Eastern Zhou dynasty
Bronze
19 x 13 x 8½ (48.2 x 33.0 x 21.1)
Gift of Mr. and Mrs. Eli Lilly 60.65

Large, ancient Chinese bells had no clappers but were struck on the outside to produce sounds. Recent excavations reveal bells often were made in graduated sets, with bells of various sizes creating a wide tonal range and complete musical scale. The dragon motif used in the decor of this example seems to reflect the increasing secularization of the art of the bronze caster. No longer does this beast have the awe-inspiring, dominating presence seen on earlier objects, which were used solely by the ruling elite for ceremonial purposes. During the Eastern Zhou dynasty, expensive bronzes frequently were made as utilitarian items for the wealthy or merely as a display of wealth. The dragon motif is often creatively fashioned as a rhythmic linear pattern, so intricately intertwined that it is difficult to separate the tangled bodies.

Female figure, 206 B.C.-9 A.D.
Western Han dynasty
Painted earthenware
23¾ x 9¹³⁄₁₆ x 2 ¹⁵⁄₁₆ (65.4 x 25.0 x 7.5)
Gift of Mr. and Mrs. Eli Lilly 60.74

Sculptured tomb figurines eventually replaced human sacrifices prevalent in earlier burials, perhaps reaching a highpoint in the excavated, life-sized ceramic figures from the tomb of the first emperor of the preceding Qin dynasty (221-206 B.C.). On this graceful Han dynasty lady can be seen the traces of original black, red, and brown painted details used to highlight her face and robes. With a slender body, knees slightly bent, and flowing robe, the figure evocatively represents the more ethereal ideal of beauty popular during this early formative period of Chinese culture.

Lion stand, late 3rd century A.D.
Western Jin dynasty
Stoneware with green glaze
3½ x 4⅞ x 2 (8.0 x 12.5 x 5.1)
Gift of Keith Uhl Clary 1986.259

This object is in the shape of a crouching lion whose back is pierced by a small circular tube. Its head is thrown back with a dramatic facial expression: staring round eyes, projecting nose, and a fierce grimace with sharp teeth, similar to the near contemporary monumental lion statues guarding the fourth-century imperial tombs in southeastern China.

The function of the tube on the back is unclear. Some consider this type of object to be a candle stand rather than a water dropper or other type of vessel. Similar pieces from recent excavations allow us to date this example to the Western Jin dynasty, when many similar objects were produced with consistently high quality celadon glazes.

Standing Buddha, 10th of January, 532
Northern Wei dynasty
Bronze
6¼ x 1¹⁵⁄₁₆ x 2 (15.7 x 5.0 x 5.1)
Gift of James W. Alsdorf 55.186

During the Northern Wei period (386-534), when Buddhism first flourished in China, small figures were made in quantities to be used on portable altars or as offerings to temples; they were often inscribed and dated. This particular piece carries perhaps the earliest dated inscription alluding to the Pure Land, or Western Paradise, which was to become prominent in later Buddhist theology in China and Japan. The basic triangular framework of the Buddha and the linear treatment of the garment reflect general characteristics of Northern Wei, a major creative period for Buddhist art in China. The Buddha, with an alms bowl in his hands, stands in front of a leaf-shaped nimbus; and he is crowned with a halo of lotus petals.

Bodhisattva, 518-618
Sui dynasty
Gilt bronze
12½ x 3⅜ x 2¼ (31.6 x 8.6 x 7.0)
Gift of Mr. and Mrs. Eli Lilly 60.47

Typical Sui period stylistic characteristics are represented in this statue, which displays excellent quality of casting in the fine details of jewelry and physical attributes. Furthermore, the relaxed standing position of the Bodhisattva, with body swaying slightly to the left, enhances the sublime expression. "Bodhisattva" is the Indian term for a deity who chose to refrain from taking the final step to Buddhahood in order to help with the salvation of mankind. This compassionate deity is frequently portrayed as an attendant of Buddha.

Horse, 8th century
Tang dynasty
Glazed earthenware
26 x 31½ x 11¹¹⁄₁₆ (66 x 80 x 28)
Gift of Mr. and Mrs. Eli Lilly 60.75

Covered with the three-colored glaze that became the hallmark of the Tang dynasty (618-906), this magnificent horse captures some of the robust spirit of that golden age of Chinese culture. Its grand size indicates it came from a tomb of an aristocrat, and it must have been one of several equally grand figurines. The bold realism and sense of powerful strength portrayed in this sculpture are typical of the aesthetics during the flourishing eighth century of the Tang dynasty, when the horse enjoyed great popularity as tribute, military steed, polo mount, and hunting companion.

Melon-shaped ewer with spout, 10th century
Five Dynasties
Glazed stoneware (Yue ware)
7 x 4½ x 4½ (17.7 x 11.5 x 11.5)
Martha Delzell Memorial and Delavan Smith Funds 1985.177

After the Tang dynasty great advances were made within the
southern traditions of lightly glazed utilitarian objects (as opposed
to the thicker lead based glazes of the northern three-colored
ware). The fine gray-toned glaze and thin body, indicative of the
kilns in southeastern China, are commonly referred to as Yue
after an ancient kingdom that once ruled the region. The proportions and form of this ewer are particularly fine, for they create
handsome contours and a pleasing shape from almost any angle.
Shallow grooves over the body subtly suggest the form of a melon.

Pilgrim or cockscomb flask, 11th century
Liao dynasty
Stoneware with lead glaze
9⅞ x 5⅝ x 4⅞ (25.2 x 14.2 x 12.4)
Gift of Charles L. Freer 12.134

The Liao dynasty was founded by a nomadic people who expanded their influence throughout Manchuria and northernmost China over the period from 907 to 1124. During that time, they adapted many aspects of the Chinese culture to their own traditional nomadic way of life. This flask, a shape unique to Liao ceramics, is based upon the popular leather flask carried on horseback and is indicative of their nomadic lifestyle. Earlier examples of this type clearly reveal that the origin of the upper silhouette is the head of a rooster.

Saucer-mouth vase, 10th-11th century
Northern Song dynasty
Glazed stoneware (Cizhou type ware)
17 1/16 x 7 3/4 x 7 3/4 (43.2 x 19.2 x 19.2)
Gift of Mr. and Mrs. Eli Lilly 47.153

The term "Cizhou type ware" is applied to a wide variety of stonewares made for everyday use in northern China from the tenth-century until the present. The ware is generally characterized by the application of a white slip and a bold design of brown or black coloring created by cutting through the slip or by painting under a clear glaze. In this well-known example of exquisite proportions and design, the large peony scrolls were made by carving through the cream-colored slip to expose the darker body as background. Judging by excavated fragments with similar designs, this vase was most likely produced at the Quheyao kiln site in Dengfeng-sian, Henan Province, not far from Cizhou.

Pair of dishes, 12th century (one pictured)
Northern Song dynasty
Glazed stoneware (Linru ware)
1½ x 6⁹⁄₁₆ x 6⁹⁄₁₆ (3.8 x 16.6 x 16.6)
Gift of Mr. and Mrs. Eli Lilly 47.133, 47.134

In response to the demand for ceramics from the capital during the
Northern Song dynasty, kilns in the Linru district of Henan began
producing high quality ceramics. In these fine examples the design of a each central peony spray is so similar that they must be a
pair from the same mold. The dense patterns with tightly curved
motifs are common to many designs of the period, and the six
small notches on the rim, suggestive of floral petals, indicate the
subtle detail so often seen in the art of this period.

Bowl, 13th century
Jin dynasty
Glazed stoneware (Jun ware)
3½ x 6 x 6 (9 x 15.2 x 15.2)
Gift of Mr. and Mrs. Eli Lilly 47.131

Jun ware, like most ceramic wares, is named after the region in which it was manufactured. In this case the early Ming dynasty (1368-1644) designation for the area in central Henan Province continues to be used because it was then that the name was first applied. There is still considerable discrepancy regarding the dating of this distinctive ware, yet appreciation of its simple, abstract beauty transcends time and culture. The "one-corner" asymmetry that became fashionable during the thirteenth century, shown here in the two floating spots of bright red on opalescent blue, is a major aesthetic shift from the central, symmetrically frontal designs of the Northern Song dynasty.

Pillow, 12th century
Jin dynasty
Glazed stoneware (Cizhou type ware)
3 x 8½ x 5⅛ (7.6 x 21.6 x 13)
Gift of Drs. K. C. and S. K. Kim 82.203

By far the most popular method of decoration on Cizhou type wares, even to this day, is painting a design in either black or brown on a cream-colored slip. This ware is well represented in the Museum's collection, and the painted designs are generally quite lively and attractive. Scenes on pillow tops, whether grand landscape vistas or charming details of nature such as this flying bird, provide a vision of painting during a period from which only relatively few examples on silk and paper survive. This pillow has an impressed seal that refers to the Zhang family, a common mark, but this unique inscription has five characters, *Zhang dajia zhen zao,* "Pillow made by the great family Zhang." A fragment with the same pictorial design was excavated at the kilns of Dongaikou in the Cizian district of Hebei.

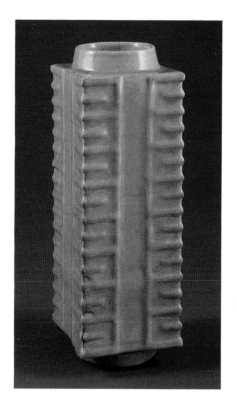

Vase, 13th century
Southern Song dynasty
Glazed stoneware (Longquan ware)
16¼ x 6 x 6 (41.2 x 15.2 x 15.2)
Gift of Mr. and Mrs. Eli Lilly 47.154

Part of the admiration for fine celadon ware – aside from its being
the oldest tradition of glazing – was due to its resemblance to jade.
This unusually large vase, which is a rectangular tube with a
circular center, is appropriately made in the form of an ancient
jade object known since the Neolithic period. Under the imperial
patronage during the Southern Song dynasty, the kilns of Longquan in southern Zhejiang produced the famous thick sea green
and bluish green glazes that are now considered the classic examples of celadons.

Bottle, 13th century
Southern Song dynasty
Glazed stoneware (Jizhou ware)
7⅞ x 3½ x 3½ (19.9 x 8.9 x 8.9)
Gift from the Collection of Sonia and Joseph M. Lesser 1985.240

Centuries ago some scholars observed that people of the Southern
Song were entirely intoxicated by the plum. Judging by poems,
paintings, records of names and even of parties, indulgence in the
delight of that flowering tree was then ubiquitous in China. One
of the preferred environments in which to enjoy the white
blossoms of this harbinger of spring was in the quiet of night,
under the moon, against the dark sky. This handsome little bottle
from the Jizhou kilns of southern Jiangxi evokes some of these
refined pleasures. Best known for their dark-glazed bowls, these
kilns displayed some of the most ingenious methods of decoration. A resist-glaze technique was used on this bottle to block out
the branch, and the finer details were added by brush.

Bimi Sanmei Dajiaowang Jing, 1301
Yuan dynasty
Wood-block print
12 x 17½ (30.4 x 44.4)
Gift of Ben Domont 1984.53

A sutra is a sermon by the historical Buddha, Shakyamuni, and it is part of the collection of sacred texts known as the *Tripitaka.* This sutra was printed using blocks, a technique that began in China during the eighth century. The production of this edition of the entire canonical collection began in 1231 and was completed in 1322. This particular section has a three-line colophon that indicates that a certain Zhu family ordered the printing of 1,000 volumes of the *Tripitaka* as an offering to the monastery for permanent circulation in the year 1301. The pictorial frontispiece, depicting the Buddha preaching, shows the overt Tibetan-Nepalese influence on Chinese Buddhist iconography during the Yuan period as exemplified by such features as narrow-waisted figures, triangular faces, and the type of throne and embellishments. The text follows the dominant style of late Southern Song carving and the calligraphic style employed for books.

Attributed to Li Kan, 1245-1320
Old Trees, Bamboo, and Rocks
Yuan dynasty
Ink on silk
62⅞ x 33¾ (159.5 x 85.7)
Gift of Mr. and Mrs. Eli Lilly 60.142

The subject of old trees by a cold stream was a theme of great antiquity even in the Yuan period. The old tree has been a philosophical symbol since the Daoist mystic Zhuang Zi observed in the 3rd to 2nd centuries B.C. that the old tree's "useless" nature was its reason for survival. Stripped away of fancy externals and left with only the bare and gnarled branches, the old tree symbolized the power to endure adversity. Its steadfastness represented the moral character of virtuous men. For the Chinese scholar-painters who utilized the evocative and expressive aspects of nature in their art, the old tree became an indirect image of the literati. The articulation of space, the clarity of the branches, the repetitive use of a restrained variety of forms, and the softness of ink tones are all stylistic qualities of the early Yuan period, when Li Kan was active. Though unsigned, the similarity of this painting to others by Li strongly supports the attribution.

Daoist Immortals, 14th century
Yuan dynasty
Ink on silk
38 x 16¹⁵⁄₁₆ (96.5 x 43.0)
Gifts of Mr. and Mrs. Ben Domont and Dan Domont 1985.190-.191

During the Yuan dynasty religious Daoism made great advances upon Buddhism, sometimes copying and incorporating whole sutras into their own body of literature by changing the Buddhist names to Daoist counterparts. The religions were affected by the syncretic environment, and the arts of both prospered from the free exchange. Hanging scrolls such as these from a larger set often depicted important or popular figures. In these paintings pairs of the Eight Immortals, rendered in great detail, stand in a shallow setting. Elements such as the overhanging motifs, light ink wash around the figures for highlight, and delightful dense patterns reveal that both religious and secular painting shared and enjoyed the enriched atmosphere from diverse sources.

Scalloped-mouth vase, 13th-14th century
Yuan dynasty
Porcelain with translucent blue glaze
9¼ x 4½ x 4½ (23.5 x 11.5 x 11.5)
Martha Delzell Memorial and Delavan Smith Funds 1985.178

Marco Polo was the first to describe ceramic as "porcelain," a term he adapted from the Italian word for cowry shell. In this piece, which is close in date to his visit to China, the tendency of Chinese craftsmen to make one medium look or behave like another is seen. The dotted background, within panels suggestive of architectural origins, continues earlier traditions of metalwork. The treatment of the peony flowers, as well as the shape of the vase itself, reflects the straightforward and often bold or archaistic tastes during the Yuan dynasty – when China was ruled by the Mongol Khans – as opposed to the elegant refinement of the previous Song court.

Octagonal vase, 14th century
Yuan dynasty
Porcelain with celadon glaze (Longquan ware)
9⅞ x 6 x 6 (25.1 x 15.4 x 15.4)
Clarence O. Hamilton and Walter E. and Mary C. Beyer
Funds 1987.45

The creative use of unglazed surfaces was a significant innovation of Yuan dynasty ceramics, and one that brought new life to the great tradition of green-glazed wares, celadons. For a tradition, then over two-thousand years old, that never used underglaze drawing, unglazed sections provided sharp definition not easily achieved under the glaze.

Each of the eight sections has panels either of chrysanthemum or peony design molded under the glaze and a rectangular molded unglazed panel depicting one of the popular Daoist immortals surrounded by clouds. Because the glaze was more refined than in earlier times, the green is more opaque and has less visual depth, but it contrasts well with the rust-brown color of the burnt body.

Cup stand, early 15th century
Ming dynasty
Porcelain with red underglaze (Jingdezhen ware)
1 x 7½ x 7½ (26 x 19.2 x 19.2)
Gift of Mr. and Mrs. Eli Lilly 60.94

Red underglaze painting with copper pigments was inspired by the blue and white wares of the fourteenth century, but the technical difficulties were never consistently mastered. Frequently, the desired red turned out to be a soft gray because the reducing atmosphere in the kiln was not strong enough. These wares soon became overshadowed by the more reliably successful blue and white wares.

The rich, even red of this stand is unusually fine, and the reserve style of decoration is quite rare in any underglaze ware. The central peony blossom, inside the raised ring that held the cup, is enclosed by a scrolling band of the *lingzhi* motif, the fungus of immortality, which in turn is surrounded by lotuses and peonies. The edge of the saucerlike stand consists of eight bracket-shaped lobes. On the underside each lobe is enhanced by two lotus petal panels that enclose a trefoil and circle motif. The only nonfloral design, a key fret band around the edge, suggests a relationship to similar stands made of silver.

Vase, (*meiping*)
Ming dynasty, Xuande period, 1426-35
Underglaze blue porcelain (Jingdezhen ware)
13½ x 8¼ x 8¼ (34.3 x 21.0 x 21.0)
Gift of Mr. and Mrs. Eli Lilly 60.82

Blue-and-white porcelain has been made since the fourteenth century. Initially, it was little valued by the Chinese, apparently having been developed for export to the Near East. During the early Ming dynasty this ware was adapted to Chinese court taste, and, in the Xuande reign the custom of using reign marks was established. In this example – with the reign mark proudly displayed on the shoulder – the painting of the dragon above a base of lotus panels is skillfully executed in different intensities of blue that create the effect of shading on the dragon scales and in the clouds. The blue pigment is of an unusual softness and depth. The combination of strength and grace in the robust form of the vase and in the forceful vitality of the painting is representative of the ceramic art of the Xuande period at its finest.

Shen Zhou, 1427-1509
Three Catalpa Trees
Ming dynasty
Ink on paper
43¾ x 16 (100.7 x 40.8)
Gift of Mr. and Mrs. Eli Lilly 60.140

"The Three Perfections," the merger of the venerated arts of poetry, calligraphy, and painting, was one of the highest forms of artistic accomplishment in traditional China. Greatly talented in all three, Shen Zhou is considered a paragon of this literati ideal. A portrait of three trees reputedly planted by the revered statesman Fan Zhongyan (989-1052), the painting is in Shen's mature style, with bold, blunt brush strokes. In the upper right Shen Zhou's sensitive poem, inspired by thoughts about the trees, reflects on the continuity of life and traditions; it is written in his characteristically forceful style with firm, emphatic strokes. The three arts, when combined by a master as gifted as Shen Zhou, can achieve a profound intellectual meaning that richly resonates beyond their individual contribution.

Wu Wei, 1459-1508
Lady Carrying a Lute
Ming dynasty
Ink on paper
49³⁄₁₆ x 24¹⁄₁₆ (125.0 x 61.3)
Gift of Mr. and Mrs. Eli Lilly 60.36

Figure painting is the oldest major genre of Chinese painting. The depiction of women, one of the more popular subjects, is often associated with literary references or mythological legend. Here, a well-matured woman's body, reminiscent of the Tang dynasty figures, is carefully, yet suggestively, conveyed through a minimum of confident brush strokes. Wu Wei's impressive skill is evident in the utilization of a wide range of strokes, from delicately thin lines for facial features, to sinuously long strokes for clothing next to the body, and short wavy brushwork for the drapery ends. He also explored successfully every possibility of ink tones, from the dense black of the hair to the pale gray of the sash. Wu's signature of *Xiao xian* or "Little Immortal," on the upper left suggests the unconventional, carefree life style for which he was well known.

Lacquer stand, 16th century
Ming dynasty
Black lacquer inlaid with mother-of-pearl
17⅝ x 13¾ x 11¼ (44.8 x 35.0 x 28.1)
Gift of Mr. and Mrs. Robert J. Shula 1985.267

Mother-of-pearl inlaid lacquer furniture was introduced during
the Ming dynasty, when the repertoire of shapes in lacquer was
greatly expanded. In addition to being decorated with inlay of
shell, gold, or silver, lacquer was also carved and painted. Lacquer,
derived from a tree sap, creates a glossy, smooth surface when
applied to a core of wood, bamboo, cloth, pottery, metal, or other
material. Because each layer must harden thoroughly between
applications – a procedure involving weeks – it often takes
months to make a single lacquer object. The shiny and plastic
qualities of lacquer, which provide waterproof protection and flex-
ibility in design, have made it an appealing medium, and the
setting of iridescent shell against black lacquer is an especially
attractive technique for decorating lacquer ware: many tiny pieces
of shell, cut in varying shapes and patterns, are inlaid to create
landscape scenes and natural forms commonly found in the decorative arts. This small stand is embellished with a luxurious scene
that possibly depicts the garden of the Immortals. The design of
cranes on a pine branch is frequently associated with longevity.

Jar with cover
Ming dynasty, Jiajing period, 1522-1566
Enameled porcelain
17¼ x 15½ x 15½ (43.8 x 39.4 x 39.4)
Gift of Mr. and Mrs. Eli Lilly 60.88

Overglaze-enamel painting on porcelains decorated with under-glaze-blue designs began in China during the fifteenth century. In the sixteenth century a more exuberant style of strong colors and bold patterns developed. Large jars, like this one decorated with golden carp among water plants, are among the most impressive pieces from the Jiajing period. A six-character reign mark, *Da Ming Jiajing nianzhi* ("Made during the Jiajing reign of the Great Ming dynasty"), is written in underglaze blue in two columns on the base.

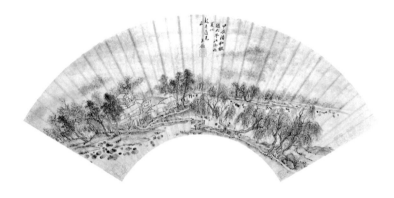

Wang Jian, 1598-1677
Landscape After Zhao Danian, 1644
Qing dynasty
Color on paper
13 x 24¾ (33.0 x 62.8)
Gift from the Collection of Sonia and Joseph M. Lesser 1983.186

The folding fan, a Japanese import in the eleventh century, has been popular in China since the sixteenth century. In China fans were used not only for cooling during the hot summer days but also as vehicles for the fine arts. Painted fans were often removed from their supporting ribs, which were usually made of wood or bamboo, and mounted as album leaves. Great artists frequently created striking images within the restrictions imposed by the fan's unusual shape. Here, Wang Jian depicted a bucolic river scene in the style of the Song dynasty master Zhao Danian (c. 1100). His written reference to the past master and use of motifs associated with Zhao exemplifies the "art historical" nature of later Chinese painting, which took as its primary subject previous art rather than contemporary nature. Wang Jian, one of the great masters of the Qing dynasty, led artists during the early years of the dynasty in advocating and codifying conservative orthodoxy in painting.

China

Vase
Qing dynasty, Kangxi period, 1662-1722
Enameled porcelain (*famille verte*)
16¾ x 7½ x 7½ (42.5 x 19.0 x 19.0)
Gift of Mr. and Mrs. Eli Lilly 60.117

Famille verte ornament, so-named after its dominant color, used transparent enamels and a predominantly green palette. On this impressive piece panels of different shapes, some of botanical silhouettes, float over a dense background of writhing dragons among peony plants. Various auspicious symbols and literati subjects are pictured within the white-ground panels to create a collage-like effect. The fine detail, great complexity of design, and juxtaposition of naturalistic and ornamental motifs are especially remarkable.

Bowl
Qing dynasty, Yongzheng period, 1723-35
Enameled porcelain (*famille rose*)
2⅝ x 5¼ x 5¼ (6.6 x 13.9 x 13.9)
Gift of Mr. and Mrs. Eli Lilly 60.110

The development of *famille rose* enamels became possible in the early part of the eighteenth century with the introduction of white to the enameler's palette. This allowed craftsmen to use enamels much as artists used European oil paints, with shading from lighter to darker colors and the application of one color on top of another. The delicacy and refinement of Yongzheng enameled porcelains are unmatched during other periods of the Qing dynasty, a peak era of technical proficiency of Chinese craftsmanship. On this bowl there are five circular medallions around the exterior, each of which contains a pair of butterflies of different species and two varieties of flowers, all painted in exquisite detail. The six-character reign mark, *Da Qing Yongzheng nianzhi* ("Made during the Yongzheng reign of the Great Qing dynasty"), is written on the base in underglaze blue within a double ring.

Brush washer and covered box, 17th-18th century
Qing dynasty
Nephrite
4 x 7¾ x 7¾ (10.2 x 19.6 x 19.6)
Gift of Professor and Mrs. R. Norris Shreve 71.11.4

Jade vessels, long considered to be among the luxuries of life, were associated with wealth and refinement. The peach-shaped brush washer with a covered box in the form of a fungus was one of the writing accoutrements found on a scholar's desk. The scholar-official held an important position in traditional Chinese society, and his desk and the implements on it were not only functional but of the finest materials and represented his achievements and prestige. This ingenious brush washer demonstrates the skill of the Chinese craftsman in making use of naturalistic forms in the design of a utilitarian object. The elements on the brush washer are both decorative and symbolic: the peach is an emblem of longevity, and the magical fungus, a *lingzhi*, is associated with immortality.

Qian Du, 1763-1844
The Purple Plantain Retreat After Tang Ying, 1814
Qing dynasty
Ink on paper
44 x 11⅞ (117 x 30.3)
Gift of the Alliance of the Indianapolis Museum of Art 1985.1

Born into a wealthy family with high political connections and a direct descendant of an esteemed Ming dynasty painter, Qian Du was a stereotypical "amateur" painter. He was a noted connoisseur of painting and calligraphy, wrote several extant literary collections, and was one of the last great traditional painters of the pre-modern period. His painting exemplified the extreme of the "art historical" nature of Chinese painting. In his inscription on this scroll, Qian states he has copied a painting by Tang Yin (1470-1523) that emulated the method of Li Tang (1050s-1130s). According to Qian, the Li Tang style was characterized by the absense of both color and the dots used for texture. Qian faithfully avoided color and texture dots to capture the flavor of Li Tang, and he emphasized the repetitive contrasts of light and dark areas, an idiosyncrasy of Tang Yin. The subtle, literary character of this hanging scroll is typical of the refined connoisseurship of the conservative artists of the Qing dynasty and reflects the continuity of tradition throughout the long history of Chinese culture.

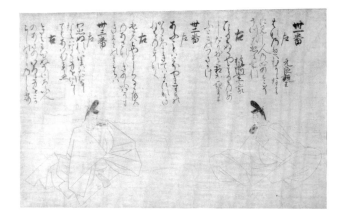

Immortal Poets
Kamakura period, 1185-1333
Ink on paper
12 x 19 (30.5 x 48.2)
Martha Delzell Memorial Fund 58.90

A favorite subject among Japanese artists over the centuries has been portraits of poets, and tradition has established several honored groupings. The figures represented here are actually sections from a longer handscroll, which depicts many poets competing in an imaginary poetry contest. This section presents two who have become legendary, Prince Motoyoshi and Councilor Iesada. Traditionally attributed to Fujiwara no Takanobu (1142-1205), the patriarch of poet paintings, this example is now considered to date to a century later and to be the work of one of a number of artists of the Kamakura period who helped to immortalize this earlier tradition. The figures are depicted in a typically Japanese fashion, with dramatic and bold yet simple patterns. The poems supposedly exchanged between them are written above their heads.

Jizo Bosatsu, 12th century
Late Fujiwara to early Kamakura periods
Joined wood-block construction
49 X 11½ X 11½ (124.5 X 29.2 X 29.2)
Evans Woollen Memorial Fund 59.29

Jizo, who is of the theological rank of a Bodhisattva (Bosatsu in Japanese), is represented here in the guise of a monk and therefore has a shaved head and none of the ornate jewelry that is characteristic of a Bodhisattva. Jizo's principal attribute is that of protector, and images of him, carved in stone, are still found along highways in Japan, where they were placed to shield travelers from harm. Stylistically, this statue reflects the transition between late Fujiwara and early Kamakura period modes of expression. The head and torso are fashioned in a highly stylized geometric manner that dominated Japanese Buddhist art of the eleventh and twelfth centuries.

Jar
Muromachi period, 1336-1573
Stoneware with ash glaze (Shigaraki ware)
17¾ x 15⅝ x 15⅝ (44.5 x 39.8 x 39.8)
Martha Delzell Memorial Fund 81.378

Shigaraki ware, named after its origin in Shiga Prefecture, was originally produced for grain storage. Because of its unassuming simplicity, however, vessels of this type won the attention of tea masters for use as water jars as early as the beginning of the sixteenth century. The tea ceremony, which originated in China, became popular in Japan as part of the meditative ritual in Zen Buddhism, and masters of the tea ceremony found the wares of everyday life especially well suited for use in seeking the simplicity of Zen. Ironically, common storage jars like this Shigaraki jar, which often have imperfections, became representations of the "artless perfection" sought in tea ceremonies.

Dish
Late Momoyama period, 1596-1615
Buff stoneware, painted iron brown glaze (Mino ware, Shino type)
2 x 9½ x 8⅛ (5.0 x 24.1 x 20.6)
Gift of the Alliance of the Indianapolis Museum of Art 1983.1

Shino ware is regarded as a uniquely Japanese expression in the art of ceramics. The production of Shino ware seems to have begun in the 1570s at the kilns in Mino. These wares were distinguished from other Japanese pottery by their heavy, rather coarse white body, and thick, cracked, uneven white glaze. The simplicity and intimacy of the shape and glaze were well suited to the tea ceremony. The shape of this dish, rectangular with scalloped corners, is common in Shino. The painting in underglaze iron shows the soft full brushwork typical of Shino. Repairs to the edges have been made with cream-colored lacquer that has golden floral designs.

Yardage from a woman's coat
Edo period, 1615-1868
Silk, satin, and twill weaves (*damask,* or *rinzu*), resist dyed
(*katazome*), embroidered with silk and metallic thread
67.7 x 63.8 (172 x 162)
Museum Accession 4893.83.1

Called the "Three Wintry Friends," the design on this yardage
depicts the pine, symbol of longevity; the plum, first to bloom in
spring; and the bamboo, strong, yet yielding. These combined
motifs pervade many Japanese art forms, and in a garment the
dramatic, bold pattern would have swept from hem to shoulder.
Certain garments were so highly regarded that they were displayed in Japanese houses on specially designed racks or during
certain seasons draped on the walls of the owners' outdoor pavil-
ions. For centuries, the complicated dyeing methods, as illustrated
in this yardage, were enormously popular in Japan. Dyeing, in
combination with embroidery, was used to produce fabric for garments that today are revered as national treasures by the Japanese.

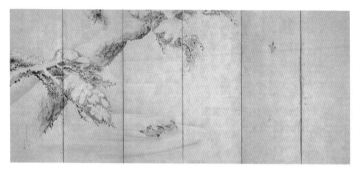

Yoshimura Kokei, 1769-1836
Heron in Willows and Ducks with Pine, 1833
Edo period
Ink and colors on gold
12 panels, 67½ x 24½ (171.5 x 62.2) each
Gift of Mr. and Mrs. Claude Warren 80.469

Kokei, a specialist in flower and bird studies, was a famous pupil of Maruyama Okyo (1733-1795), the founder of a "realist" school of painting. He was influenced both by Okyo's contact with Western art and his own interest in the naturalistic Chinese flower and bird painting of the Ming dynasty. The paintings of heron and willows with ducks swimming by a pine were spontaneously created in ink and in transparent colors that make them appear soft and light.

Katsushika Hokusai, 1760-1849
South Wind and Fair Weather
Edo period
Wood-block print
10⅛ x 15 (26.2 x 38.1)
Carl H. Lieber Memorial Fund 60.12

"Red Fuji," as this print is commonly called, is one of the finest prints in Hokusai's famous series, *Thirty-six Views of Mount Fuji*. It is a fine example of the popular woodblock prints, or *ukiyo-e*. Ukiyo-e, literally "pictures of the floating world," includes representations of things familiar and popular – courtesans, actors, city life, landscapes, nature studies, history, and literature. Hokusai's copious sketchbooks show he apparently was interested in every facet of life, but landscape remains the area in which he earned a lasting reputation. The charm of this print derives partly from its simple but striking composition: the symmetrical shape of Fuji placed off-center to the right, balanced by the deceptively intricate cloud patterns on the left. The perspective, stylized forms, and saturated color of Japanese prints such as this were a powerful inspiration to the Impressionist and Post-Impressionist painters working in Europe during the final quarter of the nineteenth century.

Kiitsu, Suzuki Motonaga, 1796-1858
Iris by Plank Bridge and *Pines*
Edo period
Ink and colors on gold
12 panels, 50 x 17½ (127.0 x 44.5) each
Mr. and Mrs. William R. Spurlock Fund 1987.43-44

Kiitsu began as a textile dyer and even invented a technique of purple dyeing. He later became a painter who revitalized the Rimpa School, a tradition that has been said to "embody the very essence of what is Japanese in Japanese art." Typically, Kiitsu here has emphasized flat shapes and bold colors, which handsomely contrast with sharp patterns and blurred ink to create strong decorative patterns.

Kiitsu's reverence for the patriarch of Rimpa, Ogata Korin (1658-1716), is revealed by the legend of his seal on the screens and the fact that in 1826 he helped prepare a publication of 100 works by Korin. The theme of iris and an eight-plank bridge is not only a reference to the famous stories about the Shinto shrine at Ise, but, in the case of these screens, is also related to similar screens by Korin, now in the Metropolitan Museum of Art, New York.

Ainu People
Woman's coat, c.1900
Bark (*attushi*) plain weave, appliquéd and
embroidered with cotton
49½ (125.7) l.
Gift of the Alliance of the Indianapolis Museum of Art 1984.221

The ethnically distinct Ainu people, who may have their origins in the neolithic Jomon culture (c. 200 B.C.), were the original inhabitants of the island of Hokkaido. This garment was produced by an Ainu woman, and its rather restrained design also indicates it was worn by a female. The curvilinear forms that embellish the coat's upper back may relate to animal forms and probably originated from ancient designs that served as magical protection for the wearer. The fabric was woven on a narrow back-strap loom and assembled into a form that is similar to rural Japanese costume. It is appliquéd with imported cotton fabric and embroidered with chain stitch around the openings and upper back.

Standing Buddha, 8th century
Unified Silla dynasty
Gilt bronze
5¾ x 2⁹⁄₁₆ x 2¼ (14.6 x 6.5 x 5.7)
Gift of Mrs. Dimitrius Gerdan 82.307

Small statues such as this played an important role in the spread of Buddhism throughout Asia. Objects made during this period of relative peace exhibit a harmonious blend of the robust Tang dynasty style imported from China with local Korean taste. The finely cast statue, with its openwork base, double lotus pedestal, and symmetrically balanced, stocky figure, illustrates the eighth-century style in Korea. As with many Buddhist figures, this Buddha exhibits symbolic hand gestures: the right hand indicates reassurance and protection, while the left hand makes a gift-conferring gesture.

Cup and stand, 13th century
Koryo dynasty
Inlaid stoneware with celadon glaze
5⅜ x 5¾ x 5¾ (13.8 x 14.5 x 14.5)
Gift of the Alliance of the Indianapolis Museum of Art 72.24.1

One of the most characteristic products of the Korean potter is the inlaid celadon ware created by filling engraved decoration with white and dark clay. This cup and stand, derived from Chinese prototypes, is fashioned in the shape of a flower with inlaid designs of chrysanthemums. Its twelve-petal form is somewhat unusual, as is the double chrysanthemum decoration on each petal. The cup sits on the stand's inverted lotus-shaped center, which is created in an eight-petal motif. The bowl of the stand has an incised wave design, and the cup rests on an incised floral pattern. The elongated proportions and greenish-gray glaze indicate that this piece followed the twelfth-century zenith of the inlay tradition in Korea.

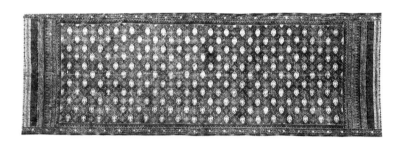

Wrapper (*phanung*), 18th century
Cotton plain weave, mordant and resist dyed
45 x 133 (114 x 337)
Jacob Metzger Fund 47.184

The Thai preferred Indian cloths made on the Coromandel Coast, and Europeans supplied Thailand with Indian textiles in exchange for skins and sappanwood for dye. Such imports exemplified by this *phanung*, are illustrated in Thai manuscripts as seating or reclining cloths, and probably also were used as wrapped garments, as their composition mirrors that of Indian saris. The intricate filigree design that appears in the borders and central field of this cloth was particularly favored by the Thai. The tracery design in the central area surrounds the torsos of the heavenly beings (*apsaras*), who make gestures of adoration.

Bed cover (*palampore*), c. 1770
Cotton plain weave, mordant and resist dyed
129 x 92 (327 x 233)
Eliza M. and Sarah L. Niblack Collection 33.1324

Bed covers with a flowering tree motif made in the Coromandel
Coast Area were a mainstay of the late seventeenth- and eighteenth-century Indo-European trade. This motif combined a "Tree
of Life," a traditional symbol used in Southeast Asian, Middle
Eastern, medieval European rites, with designs derived from European embroidery and fabric patterns, as well as from contemporary botanical books. The designs were further mixed with those
of a fashionably exotic chinoiserie flavor and sent to India, where
they were reinterpreted in spreads. Such exotic goods were eagerly
acquired by fashionable Europeans to adorn their manors and
their bodies. Later the goods were outlawed in an attempt to equal-
ize the balance of trade.

Face of Glory (*Kirttimukha*), 13th century
Gray basalt (probably from Surabaya area, East Java)
29 x 33 x 33 (73.6 x 83.8 x 83.8)
Martha Delzell Memorial and Roger G. Wolcott Funds 82.57

The *Kirttimukha* is often carved at the apex of arches in Hindu-Buddhist architecture in India and Southeast Asia. It is an adornment that is added to passageways to suggest their symbolic meanings as architectural analogies to the paths of man to God. There are several myths related to the origins of the Kirttimukha. One of the more popular relates that a demon was beheaded by the Hindu god Vishnu for stealing a drink of the elixir of immortality. The demon drank enough, however, to make its head immortal, and ever since it has been seeking to devour its betrayers. In Java the Kirttimukha is called *Banaspati*, "Spirit of the Woods," and the lionlike face is the lord and patron of the native jungle. The face here, distorted with fury, has garlands emanating from its mouth and is surrounded by vegetal forms.

Woman's wrapper (*lau hada*), 19th century
Cotton plain weave, embroidered with shells and beads
29 x 46½ (74 x 118)
Eliza M. and Sarah L. Niblack Collection 33.682

Only the highest nobility on Sumba Island owned such impressively embroidered *lau hada*. The wrapper came into the possession of a bride as part of the ritualized gift exchange that accompanied her nuptials. The male and female figures allude to fertility and the continuity of life; human, animal, and vegetal in this world and beneficent relations with ancester spirits in the next. A garment such as this rarely enters a museum collection because it was meant to accompany its owner to the grave, where it would serve as a statement of her position in the next world.

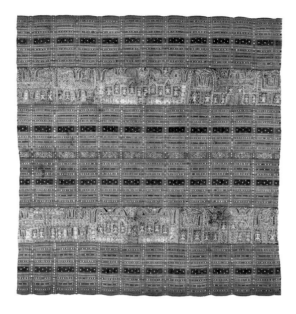

Woman's wrapper (*tapis*), 19th century
Silk and cotton plain weave with silk supplementary weft,
resist-dyed warp (*ikat*); embroidered with silk,
metallic thread and mirrors
52¼ x 51½ (132.5 x 131)
Martha Delzell Memorial Fund 82.149

Although embroidery is not a traditional method for decorating textiles in Indonesia, it was used in the Lampong region of Southern Sumatra to ornament prestigious clothing. This fabric is decorated with human figures, vegetal forms, and ship motifs that are expressive of the continuance of life here on earth and beyond. The outlined organic motifs contrast dramatically with the banded woven ground that is sprinkled with bits of mirror. This *tapis* was originally sewn into a tube, which was belted at the waist and worn as a skirt with a jacket, elaborate jewelry, and a headpiece to important ceremonial occasions.

Ethnographic Collection

Baule People
Heddle pulley, 20th century
Wood, metal, leather
11⅛ (28.3) h.
Emma Harter Sweetser Fund 80.11

In Africa many types of utilitarian objects, such as combs, stools, containers, weapons, spoons, and heddle pulleys, incorporate figurative carving. In West Africa, men's looms have one or more pulleys at the top to carry the cord or cords that control the heddles, which are harnesses to guide warp threads. This delicately carved example was probably used on the loom of a master weaver, who must have been richly paid to be able to afford a heddle of this quality and undoubtedly commissioned it from a highly skilled master carver. Most heddle pulleys were not embellished with images, and the significance of the head on this one is uncertain.

Dan People
Ceremonial spoon, 20th century (two views)
Wood
22¼ x 3⅞ x 3¾ (56.2 x 9.5 x 8.6)
Gift of Mrs. Russell Ashby 72.115

Among certain groups in Liberia there are women who, renowned for their generosity and hospitality, are honored with the title *wakede.* During periodic communal feasts they have the important responsibility for providing food and accommodations for guests. The spoon associated with this role, *wakemia,* literally "spoon associated with feasts," is used ritually to ladle out rice to guests. The prominent bowl of such feast spoons has been compared to a "belly pregnant with rice." Legs, human, and animal heads are common handle forms. Each spoon is embodied with a "spoon spirit" that aids the *wakede* in her arduous efforts.

Wall hanging (*haïti*), 19th century
Silk velvet weave, embroidered with metallic thread
66 x 167½ (167 x 424.5)
Eliza M. and Sarah L. Niblack Collection 1983.66

Since at least the sixteenth century, magnificent embroideries
such as this were made in Fez to celebrate important occasions.
This type of wall hanging was used for weddings, to hang on the
wall behind a lavishly dressed bride who was seated on an ornate
chair surrounded by sumptuous silken fabrics. Embroidery from
the Mediterranean coast of North Africa is derived from Islamic
designs which have been prevalent in the area since the early
eighth century. Here, an architectural tracery is interpreted in gold
threads on alternating panels of green and red velvet.

Shluh (Chleuh) Subgroup, Berber People
Man's cape (*akhnif*), 19th century
Wool plain weave with wool and cotton supplementary weft
wrapping; wool and silk supplementary weft knotted pile; wool
and cotton twining; embroidered with wool
66 (167) l.
Eliza M. and Sarah L. Niblack Collection 33.1984

This dramatic cape was woven in one piece and carefully shaped
during the weaving process to curve over the shoulders of the
wearer. Its dense structure made it useful as a waterproof garment
for nomadic herders in the High Atlas Region. The red oculus,
created by inserting increasing numbers of threads into the weave,
serves as a protective device to ward off malevolent influences of
the evil eye.

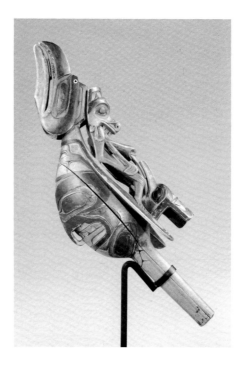

Haida People
Ceremonial rattle, 19th century
Wood, pigment
11 (28) l.
Gift of Admiral Albert P. Niblack 30.550

Rattles such as this one were part of Northwest Coast Indian shamans' paraphernalia. The carved imagery depicts Raven, the trickster-transformer, whose tales set forth rules for correct conduct and a proper relationship between the natural and spiritual worlds. In his mouth is a frog's tongue, from which Raven is sucking "poison" to empower his spells. This rattle is carved in an intricate curvilinear interlacing style, typical of Haida designs. This piece was collected in the field by an Indianapolis native, Albert P. Niblack, an early ethnographer, who wrote *Coastal Indians of Southern Alaska and Northern British Columbia* in 1887.

Index

Notes